A Coat of V

A Play Of Mu

Ronald Millar

Suggested by the novel
by C. P. Snow

Samuel French – *London*
New York – *Sydney* – *Toronto* – *Hollywood*

A COAT OF VARNISH

First presented by Duncan C. Weldon for Triumph Theatre Productions Ltd, by arrangement with Louis I. Michaels Ltd, at the Theatre Royal Haymarket, London, on 1st April, 1982, with the following cast of characters:

Frank Briers	Peter Barkworth
Lady Ashbrook	Dulcie Gray
Dr Perryman	Anthony Quayle
Loseby	Simon Shaw
Susan Thirkill	Suzanne Burden
Humphrey Leigh	Michael Denison
Sergeant Tanner	Nicholas Brent
Chief Inspector Rees	Glyn Jones
Inspector Shingler	Jonathan Coy
Professor Morgan	Charles Rea
Maria	Carmen Silvera
Police Photographer	Jeremy Stockwell
Stenographer	Petronella Ford
Policewoman	Lavinia Doran

Directed by Anthony Quayle

Designed by Finlay James

The action of the play takes place in a first floor drawing-room in a house in a square in London, SW1

PROLOGUE   A winter's night

ACT I
SCENE 1   Evening about 6.30 p.m., the previous summer
SCENE 2   Early morning, two weeks later
SCENE 3   Later

ACT II
SCENE 1   A few days later
SCENE 2   Early evening, autumn

EPILOGUE   A winter's night

Time—the present

PROLOGUE

A first-floor drawing-room in an empty house in a square in London SW1. A cold winter's night

There is a curtained alcove R, *with the curtains open revealing row upon row of books, and a door* UC *leading on to the landing which has a chair and a table with a telephone. The wall* R *of the door is gauze, opaque at present, but when transparent revealing a part of the landing and stairs to the upper floor. In front of this gauze wall stands a low table and folding screen. There are several small tables and upright chairs placed around the room, including a whatnot table* UR *and a drinks table* UL. DR *is a large, winged armchair with a small footstool and* R *of it a record player on a small table.* C *is a sofa with a table and* DL *is a small chair. A writing-desk with a telephone stands against the wall* L *and various ornaments, paintings and pictures adorn the other walls and tables*

When the CURTAIN *rises the white dust-sheets, for the moment draping the room's antique furniture, give the impression of a blur of white across the darkened stage, only partially lit by moonlight from the french windows* L, *which lead on to a balcony where a wicker chair is placed overlooking the garden below. On the wall between the windows, above the writing-desk, is a large portrait, barely discernible in the half-light, of a beautiful woman in her prime, dressed in the fashion of the early twenties. The portrait dominates the room*

Chief Superintendent Briers enters, closing the door behind him

Briers, a neat, compact man in his middle years, wearing a warm, nondescript overcoat, rubs his hands slowly, methodically against the cold. He looks about him at what will shortly be seen to be an elegantly-appointed drawing-room. He goes and turns on the portrait light, stands back and looks up at the portrait L. *Then he goes and turns on the other lights, takes out his reading glasses and address book, looks up a number, checks his watch and goes to the telephone on the desk. He lifts the dust-sheet, dials a number, coughs and waits*

Briers (*at length*) I'm at the house. Can you come? ... I'm ... expecting a development. ... Right. By the way, the heating's off. You'll need a coat. (*He hangs up, glances at the portrait, then looks about him. At length; gradually*) They say criminals return to the scene of the crime ... I've never known of one who did. ... But a detective ... a detective who can't keep away ... who haunts the place of execution ... that happens ... I can vouch for that ... (*He starts to move about the room, occasionally touching the dust-sheets and furniture, almost as though these inanimate objects were old friends who had shared with him a mutual experience and were therefore somehow a comfort to him*) Even the most difficult ... the most disliked ...

even the most hateful of men . . . or women . . . has a right to live life . . . to the last natural moment . . . which is why murder . . . wilful, deliberate murder . . . is a crime society devotes . . . all the resources of the law . . . to solving. Especially in an age of violence . . . a cruel age . . . where sudden death . . . by knife . . . or bullet . . . or bomb . . . where simple obliteration by ordinary human hand . . . may be waiting . . . for any of us . . . at home . . . at work . . . round the corner of the road . . . or on the floor of a London drawing-room. . . . (*He glances at the alcove* R) When murder happens, people who live in a violent age expect . . . no, *demand* . . . a very special reassurance . . . that the person or persons responsible . . . be called to account. . . . Which puts a particular pressure . . . on the forces of the law . . . to bring to justice the man . . . or woman . . . who murders. . . . To call him . . . or her . . . or them . . . to account . . . by all possible means. . . . All possible means *within the law*, that is. . . . Because, of course, the law itself is subject to the law. . . . On that, the law is . . . quite specific. . . . Records tend to indicate that the British murder one another rather more frequently in summer than in winter . . . the physical and the emotional temperature climb together. . . . So that those marked out for sudden death . . . at the hands of a fellow human being . . . are subject to particular risk . . . during a heatwave . . .

Fade to Black-out

The Lights come up almost immediately on:

ACT I

Scene 1

The same. Evening about 6.30 p.m., the previous summer

With the dust-sheets now removed from the antique furniture the elegant drawing-room is seen clearly for the first time. It is an elegance which is immediate but faded and old-fashioned, the room having been much lived in for many years, during which it has remained virtually unchanged. The french windows, like the curtains, are now open to the balcony and through them, from time to time throughout the play, in counterpoint to the action, drift bird-song, the hum of distant traffic, the gentle relaxing sounds of summer distilled through the haze of a London heatwave. When the Lights come up it is a really hot summer's evening with no breeze to stir the curtains. Lady Ashbrook, appropriately dressed for the weather, sits in the winged armchair DR. At eighty, she is still recognizably a late edition of the young woman in the portrait L. There is a brisk asperity about her, younger than her years. Standing beside her, taking her pulse, is Dr Perryman, a quietly-spoken, sympathetic, middle-aged man with grey in his hair. On the balcony stand a handsome young man in Army officer's uniform and a girl who seem totally absorbed in each other. They are Captain Loseby, Lady Ashbrook's twenty-nine year old grandson, and Susan Thirkill, an attractive girl of twenty-three

Lady Ashbrook (*at length*) Well?
Dr Perryman Regular. Unruffled.
Lady Ashbrook I wish I felt it.
Dr Perryman What *do* you feel?
Lady Ashbrook (*considers*) Apprehension.
Dr Perryman (*dropping her wrist*) Given the possible prognosis it would be unnatural not to feel a certain tension. And then the heat ...
Lady Ashbrook It's not the heat. . . . I've had a good run, a long run by any standard. Enough ought to be enough. . . . It's not. . . . I want to go on ... on and on ... indefinitely. . . . Absurd. Irrational. Shaming. . . . Why does one tell one's doctor what one wouldn't tell a friend?
Dr Perryman I rather hoped I qualified on either count.
Lady Ashbrook You qualify. . . . A whisky?
Dr Perryman Thank you, not while I'm on duty. (*He drifts towards the drinks table*)
Lady Ashbrook Oh my dear man ...
Dr Perryman (*pouring a drink*) A bitter lemon, then. And you?
Lady Ashbrook Give me a Coca-cola.

He pours her a drink

Ralph. No pain. All I ask is, no pain. Just . . . out.

He hands her the drink

(*Firmly*) You'll see to it — when the time comes.
Dr Perryman *If.*
Lady Ashbrook *When.* I know I'm dying. I don't care for the idea, you understand, but I *know.*
Dr Perryman In that case — without agreeing——
Lady Ashbrook Or disagreeing?
Dr Perryman — I salute your courage.

They salute each other

Lady Ashbrook There's an old military saying. German, I think. "It doesn't matter what your morale is. What matters is how you behave." My generation was brought up on it.
Dr Perryman Also — unfashionable word — your class?
Lady Ashbrook I don't reject the appellation. What is class but breeding? Still respected in a race-horse, if not in the human race. We were taught, my generation, "Never betray emotion in public." I take it your profession is similarly instructed.
Dr Perryman I don't recall it as part of the syllabus.
Lady Ashbrook Isn't the secret of the bedside manner to dissemble? To give nothing away?
Dr Perryman In your case there may well be nothing to give.

On the balcony, Susan twines her arms round Loseby's neck and kisses him lingeringly on the lips. Lady Ashbrook purses hers

(*Following her glance*) All the same, it's good to have company at such a time.
Lady Ashbrook My grandson isn't company, he's family.
Dr Perryman And the girl?
Lady Ashbrook Never. Not while I'm alive.
Dr Perryman She's not unattractive.
Lady Ashbrook Good enough for a slap and tickle. Out of the bedroom, out of the question.
Dr Perryman I don't remember seeing her here before.
Lady Ashbrook She lives across the square. Permanently horizontal, I'm told. During one of her rare vertical moments she picked him up — or he picked her up, I forget which — on one of his leaves.
Dr Perryman They look well together.
Lady Ashbrook The sheen of recently satisfied sex.

Susan giggles and once more embraces Loseby with enthusiasm

Insatiable. Those pills that athletes take to develop their athleticism . . .
Dr Perryman Anabolic steroids?
Lady Ashbrook She lives on them, I shouldn't wonder. . . . Still, tonight even

Miss What's-her-name is welcome. When sentence is about to be passed, one doesn't care to be alone.

Dr Perryman (*returning his glass to the drinks table*) You're determined to anticipate.

Lady Ashbrook And you insist on playing let's pretend. Very well, I'll play. What are the rules?

Dr Perryman Merely to keep an open mind — until we have the result of the tests.

Lady Ashbrook Is *your* mind truly open?

He hesitates

You see, you dissemble already.

A clock in the room strikes the three-quarter

That laboratory is taking an unconscionable time confirming the obvious.

Dr Perryman They have to be absolutely positive. Or positively negative. The 'phone will ring shortly. Until it does, try to believe nothing is final.

Lady Ashbrook My dear Ralph, as a medical man you are, of course, obliged to lie. You do it with an air, but unless one is naturally mendacious lying takes it out of one. Don't exhaust yourself on my account, my dear man.

Dr Perryman I assure you——

Lady Ashbrook (*putting her glass on the round table beside her*) Don't. When there's nothing to say it's best to say nothing. Pass me my cash, would you?

He takes a wad of currency from a pigeon-hole on the desk and gives it to her. She selects some bank notes meticulously and proffers them

Your usual fee.

Dr Perryman Ah, no.

Lady Ashbrook Take it.

Dr Perryman There's no urgen——

Lady Ashbrook Take it — while the going's good.

Dr Perryman I hardly think a delay of——

Lady Ashbrook Doctor, unless you're determined to raise my blood pressure beyond the safety limit, kindly take what's due to you.

Dr Perryman (*taking the money*) My grateful thanks.

Lady Ashbrook No. No, mine to you, Ralph. My very grateful thanks — for all your many services down the companionable years. Which reminds me, one last favour. When it happens — in a month, two months, whenever — I'm to be cremated and my ashes disposed of by the local vicar. There's to be no commotion, no fuss of any kind. You follow?

Dr Perryman I take it your solicitors——

Lady Ashbrook Have their instructions. But you know what England's like today: even the most traditional firm's awash with every colour of the rainbow. It only needs some no doubt worthy but quite unpronounceable Asiatic to be handling one's affairs and one could find oneself being scattered over Bangladesh. (*As an instruction*) You'll see to things.

Dr Perryman My dear Madge——

Lady Ashbrook Do I or do I not have your undertaking?

Dr Perryman But surely your grandson——
Lady Ashbrook No. No, not Loseby. You. Well?
Dr Perryman (*at length*) Should the eventuality arise.
Lady Ashbrook Good. Then it's settled.

Loseby and Susan stroll in from the US *french window*

Loseby What is settled, Grandmama? (*He pours himself a drink*)
Lady Ashbrook (*putting the money in her bag*) The anticyclone over the Azores—responsible, I gather, for the present heatwave.
Loseby Amazing, isn't it? I thought the sun had given England up as a bad job, like everyone else.
Lady Ashbrook It seems, before we sink strike-bound and riot-torn into the oil-infested waters of the North Sea, there's to be one last breathless summer.
Loseby Who says so?
Lady Ashbrook A man in Bognor Regis who predicts these things. According to *The Times* he's never wrong.
Susan (*sensuously*) A long hot summer. Lovely.
Lady Ashbrook Is it? I'm not so sure. Grey, cold and wet are what we're born to. All this sun beating down tends to make London almost sinister.
Dr Perryman Sinister?
Lady Ashbrook Street after street littered with those dreadful black plastic bags the dustmen leave when they fly off to their villas in Ibiza.
Susan Do they really have villas in Ibiza?
Loseby (*getting some ice for his drink*) No, of course they don't.
Lady Ashbrook Well, it may be Monte Carlo.
Loseby Whatever the sun does to London, it's a damn sight better than being in Frankfurt, looking down the wrong end of an SS-twenty.
Lady Ashbrook Oh, I don't want to talk about the Russian Army. And you'd better change into mufti before someone takes a potshot at you. That is, unless Miss—er——
Susan Thirkill. But please call me Susan.
Lady Ashbrook Unless Miss Thirkill insists on uniform.
Susan He looks very handsome in it, don't you think?
Lady Ashbrook Loseby looks handsome in anything, or, for that matter, nothing. But I don't have to tell *you* that, do I? (*Introducing*) Miss Thirkill—Dr Perryman.
Dr Perryman Good-evening.
Susan Hi.
Loseby How is she, Doctor?
Dr Perryman As you see, irrepressible.
Lady Ashbrook I never felt less—— (*She spots the bouquet of lilies on the* DL *chair*) Where in God's name did those come from?
Susan (*going and picking up the bouquet*) I bought them, Lady Ashbrook. They're lilies. (*She takes it to Lady Ashbrook and shows it to her*)
Lady Ashbrook (*at length*) A fraction early for the funeral. However, no doubt if they're tended carefully . . .

Susan They're meant to cheer you up. (*She goes and puts the bouquet on the desk*)

Lady Ashbrook But I'm not despondent. I'm going out not with a whimper but a bang. I'm having a fiesta, doing the things I've always most enjoyed doing, concerts, Covent Garden, Henley, for the last time.

Loseby (*going to Lady Ashbrook*) Last time nothing. I'll lay you six to four you get a clean bill.

Lady Ashbrook Don't waste your money, boy. I never do.

Loseby Except when you lose to me at Gin.

Lady Ashbrook And don't count your cards before they're dealt. You're about to get your come-uppance after dinner.

Loseby (*going to the drinks table*) I'm sorry, dear. I'll stay till seven. Then I really must go.

Lady Ashbrook Nonsense. You're dining here. And then you'll take your beating like a man.

Loseby I have a date.

Lady Ashbrook looks at Susan

Susan Not with me.

Loseby I'd get out of it if I could.

Lady Ashbrook And what disreputable assignation have you in mind tonight?

Loseby (*going and sitting on the sofa*) Did you really talk about assignations in your wicked days?

Lady Ashbrook We didn't talk half as much as your friends do. We should have thought it took the edge off things.

Loseby Oh, we talk about bed. Loudly. It's only if one's thinking of something really scandalous like getting married that it has to be whispered.

Lady Ashbrook And are you thinking of it? Marriage?

Susan is watching Loseby with equal interest

Loseby (*at length*) When I do you'll be the first to know.

Lady Ashbrook I doubt that, unless you take up table-rapping.

Humphrey Leigh appears on the balcony. He is a distinguished-looking man in his early sixties, with a touch of the military about him

Humphrey. How nice.

Humphrey (*coming in*) I hope I'm not intruding.

Loseby Hello, Humph! (*He rises and goes to the drinks table*)

Humphrey Why aren't you defending Europe? (*He crosses to Lady Ashbrook*) I slipped in through the garden door.

Loseby Ah, the famous garden door.

Humphrey In case you were asleep.

Lady Ashbrook In this? My dear, one can only swelter. What's the forecast?

Humphrey No change. They say it's going to last.

Lady Ashbrook I envy it.

Humphrey Any news?

Lady Ashbrook We're waiting for the telephone. Pointlessly, but to please Dr
Perryman I'm pretending otherwise. You know each other?
Dr Perryman By sight, I think.
Humphrey By reputation. (*To Dr Perryman*) She's in good hands.
Dr Perryman Thank you. (*He sits*)
Lady Ashbrook Don't say that, he'll up his charges. Loseby, give Humphrey
a drink.
Humphrey Something soft.

Loseby fetches Humphrey a drink

Lady Ashbrook Oh, this is Sheila Thurston.
Susan Susan Thirkill.
Humphrey Humphrey Leigh. How do you do.

They shake hands

Susan I'm fine, thanks. Why famous?
Humphrey I'm sorry?
Susan The garden door. Why famous?
Humphrey The story is that eminent Victorian gentlemen used it, to slip
discreetly in and out.
Susan Why?
Lady Ashbrook (*rising and going to the french windows*) It really is quite
excessively hot in here. Shall we go out on to the balcony?
Susan Why? What were they up to?
Lady Ashbrook Since you press the point, whatever men do, or rather did,
get up to in what was said to be London's best and most distinguished
brothel.
Susan (*delightedly*) A brothel! But I've never been in a brothel.
Lady Ashbrook Is that so?
Susan Oh, but that's fantastic!
Lady Ashbrook I'm afraid there are no vacancies. We're no longer trading.
Loseby (*moving to Lady Ashbrook*) And was it, Grandmama?
Lady Ashbrook Was it what?
Loseby London's best and most distinguished?
Lady Ashbrook My dear boy, I have no idea. Even I am not a hundred.

*She goes on to the balcony escorted by Loseby and Susan. They seat her in the
wicker chair, facing the garden. She fans herself. Dr Perryman is studying his
diary*

Humphrey (*crossing to Dr Perryman*) . . . How is she? Truthfully? I'm more
than just a neighbour.
Dr Perryman Second cousin isn't it? I asked for names to get in touch with, in
an emergency. Her son being permanently abroad.
Humphrey They don't get on.
Dr Perryman So I gathered.
Humphrey I don't know if you'd care to tell me what her chances are.
Confidentially. I'm used to secrets.
Dr Perryman Yes. You were . . . in that particular service, I believe.

Humphrey She told you that, too?

Dr Perryman Only after you'd retired. I'm afraid women chat as freely to their doctors as to their hairdressers, Colonel.

Humphrey Retired, as you say. What hope is there?

Dr Perryman (*delicately less than optimistic*) One can't be sure until one sees the plates. However . . .

Humphrey nods. Pause

Humphrey An unpleasant way to die.

Dr Perryman There are quite a number of unpleasant ways.

Humphrey I've seen one or two . . . I think, in her shoes, if the worst came to the worst, I should expect my doctor to . . . ease me out.

Dr Perryman Should you now? Well, you wouldn't be the first relative who has said that.

Humphrey And I take it you're not the first doctor who's listened? She shouldn't live here alone, with just a daily coming in.

Dr Perryman I've told her so a dozen times. She has an independent mind.

Humphrey And a powerful will.

Dr Perryman Very.

Susan comes in from the balcony

Susan She wants the lilies in a vase — to remind her. (*She picks up the bouquet and goes to the* US *door*)

Dr Perryman Of what?

Susan Time's winged chariot or something. Lilies. God, I should have thought.

Dr Perryman Don't let it bother you.

Susan It doesn't. It's just that Mister will think I'm such a burk.

Dr Perryman Mister?

Susan Loseby.

Humphrey Anyone who thought that would be . . . something of a burk himself . . .

Susan Vases in the pantry. Now where's . . .?

Humphrey Through that door, first on the left. (*He goes to the drinks table and puts his glass down*)

Susan Thanks.

She starts out and stops as a distant bell rings

Lady Ashbrook (*sharply, from the balcony*) Was that the telephone?

Dr Perryman Next door, Madge. Excuse me, Colonel. (*He goes on to the balcony*)

Susan (*coming down to Humphrey*) Can I ask you something?

Humphrey By all means.

Susan (*sitting on the sofa*) You're a sort of relative, aren't you?

Humphrey Yes.

Susan And you've known Mister for years.

He nods

Well what I want to know is, am I doing it all wrong?

Humphrey It?

Susan You see, I've been sleeping with him since we met.

Humphrey (*politely*) Oh yes?

Susan He likes it and I'm good at it so we're both on a super high. But I sometimes wonder if I shouldn't play hard to get. The trouble is I'm not and everyone knows it. It's not lust. Pure and simple joy and pleasure. I seem to have an endless capacity for sex.

Humphrey That ... must be exhausting.

Susan No, but it's a fearful bore. Would you say I was a nympho?

Humphrey I'm hardly qualified to express a view.

Susan I do like Mister. I mean, really like him, not just bed. It's just possible it could be serious. That would be a lark. There's more to Mister than appears, you know. Or perhaps you don't. He's not just Army. He gets bored easily. I'll have to watch it. (*She rises and goes and looks at the twenties portrait of Lady Ashbrook*) Watch her, too — while she's still with us. She's a sort of museum piece really, isn't she? And, golly moses, she lives in one. It's sort of creepy twenties' time, isn't it? She disapproves of me. I can't think why. We've lots in common. She was a goer in her day, wasn't she?

Humphrey Again, I'm ... hardly qualified——

Susan I am. It takes one to know one. (*She exits with the flowers*)

Humphrey looks after her. Loseby appears quietly in the DS *french window*

Loseby What do you think?

Humphrey She's ... charming ... articulate ...

Loseby (*going to the drinks table*) Oh, come on, Humph.

Humphrey Is it serious?

Loseby (*grinning*) You know me.

Humphrey Do I?

Loseby No, of course it's not serious. She lives just round the corner. It's ... convenient.

Humphrey And that's all there is?

Loseby You'll be relieved to hear.

Humphrey I didn't say so.

Loseby You don't have to. ... (*He goes and sits on the sofa*) I suppose it's all U-P with grandmama? Bloody shame. Another bit of old England down the plughole. Not everyone will weep, of course. All the same ...

Humphrey You came over specially?

Loseby No. We're playing a team from Brazil tomorrow on Smith's Lawn, and I had to see her, didn't I? Just once more. In father's unlamented absence ... I shall miss her.

Humphrey Yes.

Susan returns with the lilies in a vase

Susan Where shall I put them? (*She goes to the desk*) Here? Or is it too crowded?

Loseby Fine.

Susan (*going to the whatnot table*) Or would here be better? No, that's got flowers on it as well.

Loseby It doesn't matter.

Susan I know—how about here? (*She goes to the* US *table and puts the vase down*)

Loseby Sue, for Christ's sake! Put the bloody things anywhere you bloody like! It couldn't matter bloody less!

The telephone rings

(*Answering the telephone*) Yes? . . . I'll get him.

Dr Perryman appears from the balcony

Loseby holds out the receiver and Dr Perryman takes it

Lady Ashbrook (*quietly, standing in the opening to the balcony*) Ralph. Take it on the landing.

Dr Perryman looks at her and goes out, leaving the door open

Dr Perryman (*off*) Dr Perryman. . . . Yes . . . go ahead.

Lady Ashbrook Humphrey. Close it.

He hesitates

Close the door.

Susan does so. Lady Ashbrook picks up the receiver, as though about to put it to her ear, hesitates, and firmly replaces it. She goes to her chair DR *and sits*

(*Lightly*) Yesterday, I went to Henley. I've always adored the Regatta, it's so absurdly English. The women going around practically naked while the men die of heatstroke because they mustn't take their jackets off. . . . The Band of the Grenadiers pumping out *The Yeomen of the Guard* under a blue-and-white striped awning . . . men with that ferocious red complexion you only see in one of Turner's more abandoned sunsets. . . . Youths in flannels and multi-coloured blazers—I wonder, would someone be kind enough to give me a small brandy?

Loseby goes to the drinks table and brings the decanter and glass to Lady Ashbrook and quickly pours her a brandy

Thank you. (*She sips the brandy*) Where was I?

Humphrey Blazers at Henley.

Lady Ashbrook There's something reassuring about a blazer.

Loseby takes the decanter back to the drinks table

Like the chorus of that nigger minstrel show on television that goes on forever. Or has it stopped now?

Pause. There is the ping of the telephone receiver being replaced in the hall. A moment

Dr Perryman returns

(*To Dr Perryman*) Now then, Ralph. Out with it. We all know what you have to tell us.

Dr Perryman (*going to Lady Ashbrook*) No, you don't. It's all right. ... You're all right.

Lady Ashbrook What was that you said?

Dr Perryman They can't find anything. No sign at all. (*He grasps both her hands in his; warmly*) You're in the clear.

Lady Ashbrook But—are you certain?

Dr Perryman The report is unequivocal. There's no clinical doubt whatever.

Lady Ashbrook (*dazed, trying to adjust*) How extraordinary. I had the most powerful premonition ...

Loseby ⎤   ⎡ (*galvanized, going to Lady Ashbrook*) What did I
      ⎟   ⎟ tell you? *What did I tell you?* (*He envelops her in a*
      ⎬(*together*)⎨ *crushing embrace*)
Humphrey ⎟   ⎟ My dear, that's the most wonderful news!
Susan ⎦   ⎣ Well done, Doctor! Congratulations.

Dr Perryman Nothing to do with me.

Lady Ashbrook (*to Loseby*) Careful, careful! Having only just been reprieved I prefer not to be asphyxiated.

Loseby starts out at the double

Where you are going?

Loseby Off-licence! For a bottle of the widow! Half a dozen bottles of the widow! Come on, Sue!

Susan Coming!

Susan and Loseby run off

Quick pause

Lady Ashbrook It seems excessive just for surviving. (*She sits again in her chair* DR) Still, I suppose it's not every day that Death taps one on the shoulder and then decides he's made a mistake.

Loseby returns

Loseby Er—rather short of the ready. Mess bills. Can I stick it on your account?

Lady Ashbrook I have no account, dear boy. You know I always pay cash.

Loseby In that case, if someone could see their way clear to ...

Humphrey (*taking out his wallet*) Allow me.

Dr Perryman (*following suit*) Yes, I——

Lady Ashbrook No. (*She takes the wad of currency from her bag, peels off a note and hands it to Loseby*) Here.

Loseby I say, that won't push the boat out very far.

Lady Ashbrook One bottle will do nicely.

Susan (*off*) Come on, Mister.

Loseby shrugs and goes

Lady Ashbrook Well. . . . For once I'm not entirely sure what to say. . . . Yes, I am. (*She raises her glass*) My very good health!

As she downs her brandy at a gulp:

Black-out

In the darkness "The Emperor Waltz" is heard, as it is between each scene throughout the play. The music is eventually drowned by a police car siren, building and screaming to a climax

SCENE 2

The same. Early morning, two weeks later

The screaming police siren suddenly cuts out

The Lights come up on the empty drawing-room. The upstage french windows and curtains are open and the early morning sun which streams in reveals a measure of havoc. Chairs are overturned, the sofa has been moved, tables are in disarray, the alcove curtains pulled down, etc. The impression is of a room partially ransacked, of violence let loose

Chief Superintendent Briers enters, carrying a briefcase, followed by Chief Inspector Rees and Inspector Shingler, who, like Briers, are in plain clothes. Tanner, a uniformed police sergeant with a walkie-talkie, comes in behind them. Briers stops dead. No-one moves. He stands for a long moment, taking in the room

Briers (*at length*) Windows?
Rees Found them open. Just like that.
Briers Photographer?
Rees On his way.
Briers Fingerprints?
Rees This room done. They're upstairs.

Shingler crosses to the alcove and stares down at something offstage. He retches and turns suddenly away, nauseated. Briers puts his briefcase down on the sofa and moves to the alcove. He stares

Briers (*at length*) The sweet corrupt smell of a dead body in a heat-wave. Who found her?
Rees The daily woman. Maria—er——
Tanner (*consulting his notebook*) Maria Constantina Caterina Fereira.
Briers Portuguese?
Rees Spanish.
Briers Who called the Station?
Rees A neighbour. Some sort of cousin. He's downstairs, drinking coffee.
Tanner And doing *The Times* crossword, sir.
Briers Cool.
Tanner How about you, sir?
Briers I do my best not to get excited, Sergeant.

Tanner No, sir. Coffee?

Briers Would be very welcome.

Tanner slips out

Shingler goes to the desk and then the record player and starts making notes

(*Without moving*) Anyone else in the house?

Rees (*shaking his head*) No. (*At length*) Not a pretty sight.

Briers No. (*He moves away from the alcove and stares up at the portrait on the wall*) She *was*, though, in her day.

Rees Society between the wars?

Briers Between, during and after. She cut quite a figure in a little world. (*Moving about the room, getting the feel of it*) There was some public work later. President of Conservative Women's Association, fifty-nine to sixty-three, Anglo-Austrian Society, Cardiac Research Trust.

Rees (*with an edge*) You knew her?

Briers (*politely*) Looked her up in *Who's Who*.

Rees (*stiffly*) *Who's Who*? Oh, yes.

Briers (*gently*) Calling the Yard in wasn't my idea, Chief Inspector.

Shingler moves about making notes all the time

Rees Or mine, Chief Superintendent. We could have handled this perfectly well locally.

Briers I don't doubt that for a moment. I'm as reluctant to be here as you are to have me. (*He coughs*) I was clearing my desk.

Rees Yes, I heard you were handing over the Murder Squad. Reasons of health?

Briers I'll be all right out of London. (*He coughs*)

Rees Your last case, then.

Briers Hopefully.

Rees I take it you'll be operating out of Gerald Road?

Briers We'll try not tread on your toes too much.

Professor Morgan comes in carrying a black case. He is a heavily-built man, cheerful, florid, sweating

Morgan Sorry I'm late, Frank.

Briers You always are.

Morgan (*going to the sofa*) Bloody traffic. One of these days our not-so-merry metropolis is going to seize up and the whole shooting match come to a lung-congested, cancer-cooking standstill. (*He puts his case on the sofa and opens it*) I suppose everyone's made a mess of things as usual?

Briers Oh yes, our prints and traces are all over the place. Professor Morgan, Home Office. Chief Inspector Rees, Gerald Road.

Rees (*stiffly*) Nothing has been touched, Professor.

Briers Norman you know.

Morgan nods to Shingler, grunts and takes off his jacket

Morgan Too hot for homicide. Still, I suppose we'd better get on with it.

Where's the—ah. (*He pulls on a pair of surgical gloves, takes an anal thermometer from his case, crosses to the alcove and stares down*) Had her picture taken, has she?

Briers Not yet. He's coming.

Morgan disappears into the alcove

Chief Inspector, perhaps you could hurry up that photographer of yours.

Rees Yes, sir. We *are* short-staffed, sir. Our regular man's on holiday. (*He starts out*)

Briers (*moving to the portrait*) Oh? Where did he go?

Rees Costa del Sol.

Briers Hardly worth it. More *sol* here.

Rees exits

Briers stares up at the portrait. He is held by it

She was young when Rupert Brooke was young.

Shingler (*disinterestedly*) Oh yes?

Briers Rupert Brooke, Julian Grenfell, Raymond Asquith. . . . Before your time, Norman.

Shingler Just a week or two, sir.

Briers She survived. The young men didn't but she lived on. Part of an England long since dead.

Shingler Different worlds, sir.

Briers Yes indeed, Norman.

Morgan re-emerges from the alcove and shakes down the thermometer. He goes to his case and take out a polythene bag into which he puts the thermometer and gloves. He replaces this in the case

Morgan Maggots are hard at it. (*Getting a cassette recorder from his case*) First name?

Briers Madge. Madge Hermione.

Morgan (*switching on the recorder and murmuring into it*) Ashbrook, Madge Hermione, deceased. (*He goes to the alcove entrance*) Cadaver on floor of alcove. Alcove adjoins living-room. Blood on carpet. Not too much. Like someone spilled half a glass of Beaujolais. Eyes open, fixed, staring. Skirt up over knees. Bloody good legs for—(*he switches off the recorder*)— what—seventy-five?

Briers Eighty.

Morgan She kept her figure. . . . (*Recording again*) Age—eighty. . . . Along top of head bisecting forehead and projecting eight/nine inches outwards—a hammer. Claws of hammer penetrated skull and brain. . . . (*He switches off the recorder*) Looks like a new form of hat, doesn't it? Create quite a stir at Ascot, that would. . . . (*Recording again*) Maggots in residence. Probably first and second generation larvae. Two blows to the head. Second would have killed her if she hadn't been dead already. (*He switches off the recorder and goes to the sofa*) Far as I can go until we cut her up.

Briers (*sharply*) What was that? Dead already. (*He goes to the alcove entrance*)

Morgan My God, why aren't you coppers given a course in medicine? (*He tosses the recorder into his case*) Look at her face, man. The spots on the cheek and neck, the eyelids.

Briers Strangled?

Morgan (*nodding*) Almost certainly from behind. (*He sits on the sofa and makes notes*) There was a bit of a struggle, a couple of bruises. I shall want the usual holiday snaps.

Shingler But the hammer — the hammer claws in the skull——

Morgan Done after death.

Briers How long after?

Morgan Hard to say. Not a lot of blood. Could be soon — even very soon after.

Briers Someone in a frenzy?

Morgan That's your department.

Briers And it happened where she's lying now? She wasn't moved after death?

Morgan From the blood on the deck it doesn't look like it. I'd say whoever did it strangled her, then stove her head in and beetled off.

Shingler (*under his breath*) Jesus.

Morgan As you say. Still . . . eighty. She might have managed a few more summers. On the other hand, could have popped off any day.

Shingler Not like this.

Briers No. A hideous way to go.

Morgan Not everyone would choose it. All the same, over fast. Our ancestors lived with violence and sudden death more sensibly than we do. Part of their daily diet. The way things are going could be part of ours soon. Society's coming apart at the bloody seams. . . . Well, nothing more I can do until I get her on the slab. Send her over when you've done with her. And don't forget the pretty pictures.

Rees returns

Briers Photographer?

Rees Stuck in a traffic jam.

Morgan Ha!

Briers Taffy. Time of death.

Morgan (*putting on his jacket*) Can't be certain till I've cut her up. But I'd say she's been dead about thirty-six hours, plus or minus three or four.

Briers Today's Monday. That takes us back to Saturday.

Morgan Well done.

Briers Evening?

Morgan Evening or night. Not before seven, not much after eleven. (*He picks up his case and moves* US) When we get her opened up we may get a little closer.

Tanner enters, followed by Maria who carries a cup of coffee for Briers on a salver

Then again we may not. (*He takes the coffee and gulps it down*) Of course, if one of your chaps comes up with an eye-witness that could pin it closer. (*Putting the cup back on the salver*) What was that?

Tanner Coffee, sir.

Briers Mine.

Morgan I did you a favour.

Morgan exits

Briers Get her covered up now, please. . . . And, Sergeant, perhaps you could move that screen across the alcove.

Tanner does so. Maria turns to go

No. You——what's your name?

Maria Maria Constantina Caterina Fereira.

Briers Please sit down.

Rees takes the salver from her and puts it on the US *table. Maria reluctantly goes and sits on the sofa, scared*

It was you who found Lady Ashbrook?

Maria (*crossing herself*) Si.

Briers What time was that?

Tanner exits

Maria (*indicating Rees*) I tell this man.

Briers Tell me.

Maria I come to work seven and a half——

Briers Seven-thirty. That's an early start.

Maria How I live? How I live without early start? Listen. When I come this country, before twenty years, I just have the one work. One. OK fine. Money is enough. Today—how many work I have today? Four. Four work I have today and still not enough money. What happen to money, please?

Tanner returns with a plastic sheet and goes into the alcove

Briers It's a long story.

Maria Is disaster.

Rees You could always go back to Spain.

Maria España? Disaster too. You know what I say? Bring back Franco.

Briers That could be difficult. Maria, when you arrived this morning, was everything downstairs in order?

Maria To begin, same as ever everything. Except—no, is nothing.

Briers What is nothing?

Maria Garden door. Always my lady lock at night. Today garden door is open. I think my lady forget to shut. I shut.

Rees You didn't tell me that.

Maria You didn't ask.

Briers Er—Chief Inspector—perhaps you would be good enough——

Rees Her prints will be all over it.

Rees goes out through the french windows

Tanner comes in from the alcove

Briers Norman. (*He nods to Shingler to follow Rees*)

Shingler follows Rees out

And I want to see that cousin, Sergeant.
Tanner Yes, sir.

Tanner exits through the US *door*

Briers (*to Maria*) Right. You shut the garden door. And then?
Maria Put on kettle, come up here.
Briers Why?
Maria To open curtain, open window. Everywhere hot — hot like oven. Then
. . . (*She shudders, looks at the alcove and crosses herself*) I think I faint. I am
strong. I no faint. I telephone.
Briers But not the police. Why not?
Maria English. My English. Very bad.
Briers After twenty years?
Maria Ever you go to Spain?
Briers Many times.
Maria How good your Spanish?
Briers (*at length*) So you rang Lady Ashbrook's cousin.
Maria Is English gentleman, Meester Leigh. Very peace. Very calm. Not
many left.
Briers Leigh. Christian name?
Maria Maybe Christian, maybe not. Is good man.

*Humphrey Leigh enters carrying a copy of "The Times" neatly folded under
his arm*

Humphrey (*cool, relaxed*) Good-morning, Frank.
Briers Humphrey! Well, I'm damned!

They shake hands

Humphrey I'm glad it's you they sent.
Briers (*with great warmth*) Good to see you. More than good. Fortuitous.
(*Suddenly*) Or was it? You didn't ask for me by any chance?
Humphrey I may have dipped a toe in the water.
Briers Why?
Humphrey Horses for courses. It seemed to me the case called for someone
who would know the social form. Also not entirely stupid.
Briers Thank you.
Humphrey Not at all.
Briers (*to Maria*) Maria. Just one more question.
Humphrey Do you want me to go?
Briers No, no. Maria, was anything missing from the house?
Maria Is some silver gone. Silver dishes. Dining-room. Small. Beautiful.
Migusto mucho.

Briers You liked them?

Maria Very nice. Very pretty. Ah! Now you think Maria thief!

Briers (*urging her towards the door*) You may go now.

Maria Never I steal! *Never!*

Briers I'm sure. Thank you.

Maria (*in tears*) Nunca! Nunca! I show you my references!

Briers Sergeant, will you look after her?

Tanner leads her out and she goes muttering Spanish imprecations

A moment. Humphrey and Briers contemplate each other

Well. . . . Sorry I can't offer you a drink.

Humphrey I don't. Not any more.

Briers What? Doctor's orders?

Humphrey Good God, no! One day I just decided not to. It was a challenge.

Briers And that you never could resist, could you? Oh, I don't believe it. In Cyprus you could put us all to bed — Turks, Cypriots, Makarios himself if necessary — and still be first down for breakfast.

Humphrey It's a long time since Cyprus, Frank. You were just a chubby young copper then. Bright, but chubby.

Briers Bright enough to use the best intelligence officer on the island. And the most unscrupulous.

Humphrey All's unfair in love and war.

Briers (*amused*) You haven't changed.

Humphrey And you? Still playing it straight down the line?

Briers You make scruples sound like a misdemeanour. (*With some urgency*) Listen, Humph, this is your back yard. You know these people. What do you make of it?

Humphrey moves away and scans the room

Humphrey A burglar who went berserk?

Briers How it looks.

Humphrey Or how it's meant to look . . .?

Briers gives him a quick, sharp glance

Do burglars carry hammers?

Briers Possible.

Humphrey I'd have thought unlikely.

Briers (*contemplating Lady Ashbrook's portrait*) Did you like her?

Humphrey I think more than she liked me. We used to bicker about politics in the thirties. Spain, you know. She's never quite trusted me since.

Briers You were relatives?

Humphrey Distant cousins.

Briers Then you're not her next of kin?

Humphrey No. There's a son. He lives in Morocco. He's not been back for years. She didn't care for him. He drinks.

Briers Husband?

Humphrey Died some years ago. A permanent Under-Secretary. Rather less permanent than anticipated. One day he just collapsed over his desk in Whitehall.

Briers The perfect exit for a Civil Servant.

Humphrey In his case less than elegantly timed. His pension wasn't index-linked.

Briers They hadn't thought that up yet?

Humphrey No. It coloured her attitude to money. She became . . .

Briers Parsimonious?

Humphrey Cautious.

Briers Who was she close to? Really close? Anyone?

Humphrey Her grandson.

Briers And he to her?

Humphrey To all appearances. He was over here a fortnight ago, playing polo.

Briers Over here from where?

Humphrey Germany. He's a Captain in the Life Guards.

Tanner appears, with a young Police Photographer behind him

Tanner Photographer, sir.

Briers Come in, come in.

The Photographer comes into the room, carrying his apparatus. He is casually dressed in jeans and without a tie

Photographer (*bored, he has seen it all*) Morning.

Briers (*to Tanner*) Get on to the Ministry of Defence. Tell them I want to speak to a Captain——?

Humphrey Loseby.

Briers Captain Loseby, Life Guards, British Army, North-West Europe. Top priority short of war. Get the MOD through the Yard.

Tanner Sir.

Tanner exits

Photographer (*scarcely stifling a yawn*) Same as usual? Room first, then body?

Briers No. (*Indicating the alcove*) Body first, then garden door, then room.

Photographer Will do.

The Photographer strolls up to the alcove and exits. The occasional click of his camera and intermittent flashes accompany the following

Briers (*to Humphrey*) Cautious—in what way?

Humphrey For example, she never used a cheque book. Everyone was paid in cash. From a wad of currency she kept in the top of the desk there.

Briers (*going and examining the desk*) How much?

Humphrey Two or three hundred, as a rule.

Briers An open invitation to theft.

Humphrey She kept the number of each note recorded in a notebook. For what that was worth.

Briers There's nothing here. (*His feet strike against the toolbox on the floor beside the desk. He lifts it up carefully*) A toolbox. In a drawing-room?

Humphrey She had everything to hand in here. It was the hub of her life, this room. She seldom left it.

Briers But a toolbox — surely if some odd job needed doing she would send for a carpenter or plumber? (*He carefully examines, without touching, the contents of the toolbox*)

Humphrey Plumbers and carpenters cost money. An old woman's harmless eccentricity.

Briers Not so harmless. There's no hammer . . .

They look at each other, then at the alcove

Rees and Shingler enter from the balcony

Rees That's how he got in all right. Via the mews, over the grass and in through the garden door. The lock's been forced.

Briers Professional job?

Rees I'd say a minor villain who knew what he was up to.

Briers Norman?

Shingler No locksmith, but no casual thug. Someone handy with a knife.

Briers (*Suddenly decisive*) Right. Let's move it. Yes, I'll be operating out of Gerald Road, Chief Inspector. Get back there fast, if you'll be so kind, and set up a Murder Room. Detailed maps of the district, filing cabinets, a blackboard and every CID man you can muster. I want a house-to-house blitz, on friends, acquaintances, anyone who ever knew the old lady, which probably means half Belgravia and Chelsea. Humphrey, this is your home ground, you can help us there. In addition I want sightings of anyone out and about this area on Saturday between seven p.m. and midnight. I don't care if it's the Mayor or the Archbishop of Canterbury or the fire brigade, someone must have seen someone. Tell the boys to be polite if they can manage it. If they can't, bring me one good solid sighting, I'll look after them. I know you're short-staffed and I know it's bloody hot but the less time anyone has to fix up an alibi the better. Use the yard for reinforcements. Any questions? (*He urges Rees out*) Then don't let me keep you, Chief Inspector.

Rees goes out, poker-faced

(*He coughs. To Shingler*) Call a Press Conference for tomorrow afternoon. If we don't give them something to bite on they'll speculate.

Shingler They'll do that anyway.

Briers But along our lines.

Shingler What lines are those?

Briers No idea, I'll think of something. Find out about her Will, who gets her money. If it turns out to be Humphrey here, that could be interesting, especially if he can't account for his movements Saturday night.

Humphrey I was at home.

Briers Alone?

Humphrey Yes. Reading and watching television.

Briers What was on?
Humphrey It didn't register. It seldom does.
Briers Quite impossible to prove?
Humphrey Oh, quite.

Briers chuckles. Shingler stares hard at Humphrey

Briers (*to Shingler*) What are you waiting for?

Shingler goes out

The telephone rings

(*Picking up the receiver by the cord*) Briers. Good-morning. ... Who am I speaking to? ... Yes, I *am* asking urgently for Captain Loseby. ... I see. You're positive there's no mistake? ... I would like that very much. ... I have it. Thank you. ... And you have a nice day, too. (*He hangs up. Gradually*) Charming girl, presumably with American connections. No, Captain Loseby is not with his regiment at the moment. He's in London on compassionate leave. He flew home three days ago, when his grandmother was taken ill.
Humphrey (*getting up*) Taken ill? But, Frank, I saw her three days ago and she was as right as rain.
Briers Would I like the London address where he is staying? Yes, I would. This address. (*He goes to the door and calls*) Maria! Sergeant, would you send Maria what's-her-name up here, please?
Tanner (*off*) Yes, sir.

Pause

The Photographer enters from the alcove

Photographer Right — garden door?

Briers nods

The Photographer goes out through the french window

Maria and Tanner enter

Briers Lady Ashbrook's grandson. Is he staying here?
Maria Was.
Briers When?
Maria Before two week.
Briers Has he been here since?

She shakes her head

For example this weekend?

Another shake

You're absolutely sure?
Maria So! Now Maria tell the lie!
Briers Have you any idea where he is?
Maria Of course Maria know where he is.

Briers Then perhaps she'd be good enough to tell us.
Maria Is in Germany, with British Army. Entiende? Unnerstan'? (*She points to the photograph of Loseby in uniform on the desk*) Look, photographié. Soldier.
Briers (*going to the desk*) Thank you. That is all.
Maria Fine soldier. Fight the world. Like Franco.

Tanner and Maria exit

Briers (*studying the photograph. To Humphrey*) Known him long?
Humphrey Since he was a boy?
Briers Trust him?
Humphrey (*carefully*) I'd trust him alongside me in a war. I'm not sure I'd trust him with money, not if I hoped to be repaid. I wouldn't trust him with a girl I was fond of . . .
Tanner ⎫ (*together, off*) ⎧ Hold it! Hold it right there!
Maria ⎬ ⎨ What you do? Let him go! (*Excitedly*) Are you
⎭ ⎩ crazy? Let him go! Police!

Loseby bursts in, throwing off Tanner who is trying to restrain him. Loseby is now in mufti—jeans, open-necked shirt

Tanner (*breathlessly*) Sorry, sir. He was on the landing before I could—I don't know how he got in.
Loseby How the hell do you think I got in? With a key, man. I live here. Humph, for God's sake tell this idiot who I am.
Humphrey Lady Ashbrook's grandson. Captain Loseby.
Briers All right, Sergeant.

Tanner glares at Loseby and exits

Briers I'm sorry. Briers, Murder Squad, Scotland Yard.
Loseby Where is she?

Briers indicates the alcove. Loseby goes to it and looks down at the body of his grandmother. He turns away, shattered

(*Moving away, his back to the audience*) Oh my God. . . . Couldn't you have moved her?
Briers She had to be photographed *in situ*.
Loseby In what?
Briers Where she is.
Loseby Unfair . . . so . . . bloody unfair . . . (*turning*) . . . she was told there was nothing wrong with her . . . just two weeks—and then this . . .
Briers How did you know?
Loseby Porter at my club——
Briers Which club?
Loseby The *In and Out*—heard it on the radio . . . I need a drink. (*He starts for the drinks table*)
Briers (*at once*) No. I'm sorry. Nothing in this room is to be touched.
Loseby Oh, for God's sake, man, have a heart.
Briers In this job that's not always possible.

Loseby Would you mind immensely if I used the phone?

Briers Yes.

Loseby (*livid*) Look, whose house is this?

Briers (*calmly*) I don't know.

Loseby What?

Briers At this moment I can't say. I don't know the contents of her Will. Do you?

Loseby (*at length*) Humph. That call box on the corner. If the local vandals haven't smashed it, do me a favour. Give divisional HQ a buzz and——

Humphrey That's been done.

Loseby (*disconcerted*) Oh. You — you rang them and asked for me?

Briers Not unnaturally.

Loseby And I wasn't there.

Briers So it seems.

Loseby (*going and sitting on the sofa*) Damn. Oh well. *C'est la guerre.*

Briers Why are you in London, Captain, *this* weekend? You were here two weekends ago, to play polo. Why now?

Pause

Loseby (*to Humphrey*) I suppose I'd better come clean.

Humphrey I would recommend it. Strongly.

Loseby (*with a change of tone, to Briers*) The thing is, my dear, I needed a spot of relaxation. You understand. So I got a few days leave. My grandmother's health was an ideal — well, I don't have to tell you it's the classical excuse.

Briers But you didn't see her? You didn't visit her at all?

Loseby I did ring up.

Briers When

Loseby Saturday afternoon.

Briers What time Saturday?

Loseby About sixteen hundred hours.

Briers More precisely?

Loseby Between four and four-fifteen. Sorry. Best can do.

Briers How was she?

Loseby She said she was fine.

Briers Where were you?

Pause

Loseby (*at length*) Not too far away.

Briers Where *were* you, Captain Loseby?

Loseby I'd rather not say. Tucked up somewhere comfortable.

Humphrey With a woman?

Loseby You said it, I haven't.

Briers Is that the truth?

Loseby Do you want me to swear on the Bible?

Humphrey No. You'd do that if you were lying in your teeth.

Loseby Whose side are you on?

Humphrey Your grandmother's.

Loseby (*with immense charm*) All right. Yes. It's the truth. I'm not saying where I was exactly because it involves someone else. (*To Humphrey*) Will that do?

Humphrey Almost certainly not.

Briers You'll have to make a statement and sign it. Then we'll check it out.

Loseby You're a suspicious devil.

Briers It's my business. By the way, the Will. Do you know what's in it?

Loseby Haven't the foggiest. Why not ask your chum here? (*He indicates Humphrey*)

Humphrey I wasn't in her confidence.

Loseby I'm not sure that anyone was.

Briers Not even you?

Loseby No, she was fond of me, that's all. (*He glances at the alcove*) It was . . . mutual . . . listen, (*he gets up abruptly*) where do wills come in? I mean, this was obviously some sort of hooligan on the rampage. Well, wasn't it?

Pause

Briers You can go now. Don't leave London.

Loseby But I'm due back on duty.

Briers (*gently*) We'll arrange compassionate leave. And this time it will be genuine.

Pause. Loseby starts out, stops, turns.

Loseby Whoever did it, you *will* get him?

Briers Oh yes. You may count on that. Him or her.

Loseby (*startled*) Her?

Briers You'd be surprised what power ungovernable rage can give a person. Where will you be staying?

Loseby At the club, I suppose.

Briers Not here?

Loseby I've no wish to set foot in this house ever again.

Briers It disturbs you that much, does it?

Loseby Good God, man, would *you* want to make an empty house where murder happened *your* HQ?

Loseby strides out

A moment

Briers (*at length, to Humphrey*) What an interesting idea. It hadn't occurred to me.

Black-out

SCENE 3

The same. Later

With as little rearrangement of furniture as possible the drawing-room is now Briers' HQ. It accommodates a set of three filing cabinets against the upstage wall with a noticeboard above them. A large map of London, with various coloured areas, is pinned to the board together with other papers. In front of it is the upright chair from DR and a small desk on which stand several telephones, a typewriter and papers. The alcove curtains have been put back and are now closed and in front of them stands a large blackboard and easel to which is pinned a detailed map of south-west London with the house ringed in red. On the blackboard the words "Belgravia", "Chelsea", "Pimlico", "Victoria", "Lambeth", and adjacent boroughs are chalked up and alongside them the number of houses visited in each. The sofa is now placed R and Lady Ashbrook's winged-armchair C, next to a cloth-covered trestle table which serves as Briers' desk. The armchair is positioned so that whoever is being interviewed or questioned is forced to sit in it. On the trestle table are writing or scribbling pads, pens, pencils, an intercom telephone, and a bottle of cough mixture and a glass. The writing-desk chair is now placed behind the trestle table

As the Lights come up Dr Perryman is sitting in the winged-armchair checking his diary and Briers sits behind the trestle table. Shingler is at the desk upstage with Dr Perryman's statement

Dr Perryman ... yes, after the good news from the laboratory—that was on the seventh—I didn't see her for a fortnight—the twenty-first—and then it was just a routine call. There was nothing wrong with her that a little company couldn't cure.

Briers Quite. If you'd just sign your statement.

Shingler brings the statement to Dr Perryman

Shingler (*indicating*) There, sir.

Dr Perryman signs

Briers Thank you, Doctor. You've helped us considerably.
Dr Perryman I'm not entirely sure how.
Briers By narrowing the time still further. We now know she was fit and well when you left that evening.

Shingler exits UC

In fact you are almost certainly the last person to have seen her alive.

A Policewoman enters with a tray of food which she places in front of Briers

Dr Perryman Except for whoever took her life.
Briers Except for whoever killed her, yes. Thank you, Ann.

The Policewoman exits

Dr Perryman gets up, goes to the sofa and picks up his bag

(*Eating*) Sorry about this. Can I offer you a Scotch?
Dr Perryman Thank you but I still have several calls to make.
Briers It's bad, is it, if your patients know you've had a drink?
Dr Perryman It's not so much the knowledge as the smell. It makes them nervous.

Briers Ah.

Dr Perryman (*going to the blackboard*) I take it all this means you're making progress?

Briers It depends what you mean by progress. In a matter of days fifty-six detectives have been inside seven-hundred and thirty-nine houses, foraged in dozens of local dives and pubs, talked to all the villains in the neighbourhood we knew about and identified a host of others that we didn't. We've unearthed more of the criminal population of South-West London than you'd dream existed. In that sense, yes, we're making progress. On the other hand, if you mean are we any nearer knowing who killed Lady Ashbrook, no, I'm afraid we're not.

Dr Perryman (*coming back and sitting in the winged-armchair*) But you're convinced are you — correct me if I'm wrong — that whoever did this ghastly thing was a stranger, some sort of criminal intruder?

Briers No, I'm not convinced of that.

Dr Perryman Ah! No more am I. Of course, I'm a total ignoramus in police matters but, speaking as a medical man, when I saw her lying in the mortuary and later during the autopsy, it seemed to me . . .

Briers Yes?

Dr Perryman Well, I really have no right to express a view but if a burglar was responsible, wouldn't there have been more indication of a struggle? So far as I could tell, there was little sign of one. Hardly any pressure marks. Scarcely any bruising. I couldn't help the rather obvious reflection that she might have been killed by someone she knew.

Briers You mean someone doing his best to behave like a burglar?

Dr Perryman The thought crept up my back — or am I talking nonsense?

Briers No, it crept up my back too.

Dr Perryman Then all these conscientious inquiries, done with all the resources of the Yard, are simply a cover? You're actually looking rather nearer home?

Briers We haven't ruled out the possibility of a professional. At the same time, after years of doing this sort of work, one develops certain . . . antennae.

Dr Perryman And yours are telling you what mine are telling me?

Briers You get a feeling in your fingers. By the way, whoever murdered Lady Ashbrook either wore gloves or wiped away his prints. There wasn't a fingerprint in the house that we can't account for.

Dr Perryman What about footprints?

Briers None. He may even have gone out through the garden in his stockinged feet.

Dr Perryman Interesting. So that if he wasn't a professional he behaved like one in all respects?

Briers Not quite all. Three hundred pounds in cash gone, some silver dishes stolen — that's professional enough. He didn't need to beat her head in, though. That's not professional.

Dr Perryman The horror of it . . . the brutality . . . one can't help feeling that when we abolished capital punishment we made a serious mistake.

Briers You're a hanger, are you, Doctor?

Dr Perryman Hanging, no. Too many sexual connotations. But I believe in getting rid of certain kinds of criminals. Shooting, if you like. A terminal drug. The least messy method we can find.

Briers You don't feel it would be a throwback, that it would make society even less civilized than it is?

Dr Perryman It's a profound need of society to take its revenge on those who offend its deepest instincts.

Briers (*at length*) I've had to deal with some child murders. Beyond description. If I'd caught the people who did them and thought I could get away with it, I'd have shot them without thinking twice. I might have done the same to whoever killed this old lady. But I wouldn't string him up or go through any other sort of ritual execution. Have you ever heard the noise in a prison when someone was about to be executed? I did once, when I was just starting in the force. It might change your mind.

Dr Perryman I doubt it. You see, you're trying to keep life hygienic, in a world becoming daily more violent, more toxic. We have to find a way of ... balancing the books.

Briers An eye for an eye?

Dr Perryman Two eyes, perhaps, for one. I like to think of myself as a liberal humanist. It's becoming more and more difficult to sustain that position. ... I must go.

The intercom buzzer goes. Dr Perryman gets up

Briers (*answering the intercom*) Yes? ... In a moment. (*He replaces the receiver and gets up*) Well, thank you for your time, Doctor — and your statement. I've enjoyed our conversation. We must talk again.

Dr Perryman (*going to the door*) With pleasure.

Briers Oh, by the way, about those stolen notes. As I'm sure you know, she kept a record of each number in her notebook. It was in a locked drawer in her bedroom. We've dug into every shop in the Metropolitan area. Not one that was on her desk that night has turned up. (*He goes to the writing-desk drawer, takes out some notes and goes to the trestle table*) But two tenners that she used to pay a bill about a year ago have surfaced in a newsagent's in Pimlico.

Dr Perryman comes back to the trestle table

Quite naturally, in the normal way of business. You buy your papers there, don't you, at Barlow's, and you often pay in notes?

Short pause

Dr Perryman (*with a rueful smile*) I should have mentioned this before. Yes, I did let her pay me in currency and I took a fraction off the bill as a quid pro quo. A not uncommon practice nowadays. Will the Yard feel obliged to make a signal to the Inland Revenue?

Briers I shouldn't think so. We have rather more important things on our plate. And even if we do I'd be surprised if the Inland Revenue were all that interested in someone getting away with a little income tax. After all, the sum involved must be fairly modest?

Dr Perryman Marginal.

Briers I doubt if you'll hear any more about it.

Dr Perryman Thank you. It would be ... unfortunate if it got around. A doctor. Expected to be like Caesar's wife and so forth. And I'm told the penalties are no joke nowadays. I'm not a rich man.

Briers No?

Dr Perryman No, I've never made the money that I could have.

Briers Why was that, Doctor?

Dr Perryman Oh, you don't want to hear all about that.

Briers Yes, I do, I'm most interested.

Dr Perryman Any competent physician can get success as a consultant. And any man a class better can make his mark in what they call research. I wanted something better. I wanted to satisfy myself. In the long run, you know, that's all that matters. It may sound strange but I didn't want to make medicine just a shade more scientific. I wanted to make it a good deal less so.

Briers In what way?

Dr Perryman For example, what do we mean when we talk about the mind? Or the spirit? Or the will? How does the mind affect the body, and vice versa? Until we know the answers to those sort of questions we know nothing.

Briers Of course, there are some questions to which we may never know the answers.

Briers goes to the door with Dr Perryman

Dr Perryman Don't bother, I can see myself out. (*He exits*)

Briers looks after him for a moment and then comes back again to the table

Briers (*buzzing the intercom*) Right, Norman. (*He sits down*)

Shingler comes in and shuts the door

Thirkill here yet?

Shingler No, but Colonel Leigh is.

Briers Good, I want him.

Shingler I think you'd better read this first.

He lays a piece of paper on the table in front of Briers, who reads it

I thought you should know. That is, if you didn't.

Briers (*at length*) No. I didn't ...

Shingler Sir, I realize you're old friends ...

Briers Go on.

Shingler How much have you taken him into your confidence?

Briers I've been telling him as much, or as little, as I wanted him to know.

Shingler Does that mean you've ruled him out?

Briers I'll tell you precisely what it means, Norman. It means I'm watching him from the closest possible vantage point. I don't like it, but I'm doing it. No, I haven't ruled him out. I haven't ruled anyone out. Anyone at all.

Pause

Shingler Fair enough. (*He goes to his desk upstage*)

Briers (*buzzing the intercom*) Send in Colonel Leigh. (*Drily to Shingler*) Thank you, Norman. (*He taps the piece of paper*) And thank you for this.

Humphrey enters with a folded newspaper under his arm

As soon as that young woman arrives, wheel her in. Come in, Humphrey. Solved it yet?

Humphrey No. Have you?

Briers (*indicating the newspaper*) The crossword.

Humphrey I'm stuck at thirteen across, "Dyspeptic gathering? Question mark. More than likely." Two words.

Briers How many letters?

Humphrey Six and seven.

Briers (*brooding*) "Dyspeptic gathering? More than likely . . ."

Shingler Livery Company?

Humphrey (*surprised*) Why, yes . . . thank you, Inspector.

Shingler My pleasure.

Shingler exits

Humphrey (*filling in the crossword*) That was bright.

Briers I run a bright department.

Humphrey (*going to the blackboard*) And a thorough one. My old firm couldn't have mounted a search like this.

Briers (*holding Shingler's paper in his hand*) Tell me——

Humphrey But then we didn't have your resources.

Briers What do you know about . . . (*he changes his mind and puts the paper face downwards on the table*) . . . Dr Perryman?

Humphrey Not a lot. Those who do, speak highly of him. Why?

Briers He's been working a tax fiddle.

Humphrey I used to think most of us were honest about money. Now I sometimes think that none of us are.

Shingler enters followed by Susan. She is tanned and wearing the minimum of clothing that the heatwave and decency permit

Humphrey sits on the sofa

Shingler Miss Thirkill.

Shingler exits

Susan (*shaking hands with Briers*) Am I late? I am, aren't I? Terribly sorry but I only just got out of bed. You know how it is.

Briers (*pleasantly; indicating the winged armchair*) Sit down.

Susan Thanks. (*She sits down, immediately rises and goes to the blackboard and stares at it*) Golly, you've been busy. Are you getting warmer?

Briers (*mopping his brow*) By the minute. You don't mind Colonel Leigh being present? He's helping us with our enquiries.

Susan I say! That usually means . . . (*She goes to Humphrey; confidentially*) It *wasn't* you, was it?

Humphrey No.
Briers Please sit down, Miss Thirkill.

Susan sits on the sofa

No, no. Not over there. Come here.
Susan *Her* chair?
Briers Does it bother you?
Susan Not a scrap. Why should it? (*She sits in the winged armchair*)

Pause

Briers Well, go ahead. I'm listening.
Susan What for?
Briers You asked to see me.
Susan Oh. That's right. ... Listen, you've had Mister in three times in as
  many days, giving him the third, fourth and fifth degree. It's obvious what
  you're thinking. Well, you're wrong. It wasn't him. It couldn't possibly
  have been. Go on, ask me why. Twist my arm. All right, since you insist, I'll
  tell you. Because he was with me, that's why.

Pause

Briers (*at length; carefully*) You say Captain Loseby was with you that
  Saturday evening? (*He reaches for a file from the writing-desk*)
Susan Morning, afternoon and evening. We were together the entire
  weekend.
Briers Where?
Susan My place. Just across the Square. Don't you see? That's why he
  wangled leave. To be with me. It's always been good between us but that
  weekend, it was the best ever. We really had lift-off.

Pause

Briers And you'd be willing, would you, to swear to the truth of what you're
  saying in a court of law?
Susan (*to Humphrey*) Policemen look different when they ask you questions,
  don't they? (*To Briers*) I'd happily shout it from the house-tops.
Briers You said nothing of this at our first interview.
Susan You hadn't started bullying my boy friend, had you?

Pause

Briers Will that be all.
Susan All?
Briers Is there any further evidence you'd care to volunteer?
Susan I can't think of a thing. I just wanted to set the record straight. I felt I
  owed it to Mister. You won't tell him I told you, will you?
Briers Why not?
Susan He wouldn't want it bandied about. One of his other birds might get to
  hear.
Briers I see. What you've just described to us is not ... an exclusive
  arrangement?

Susan Lordy, no. He plays the field. We both dᴖ. (*Indicating the portrait*) That's why she didn't care for me.
Briers You disliked her?
Susan I could live without her. She stood between me and Mister. But I didn't kill her, if that's what you're thinking.
Briers (*quietly*) You couldn't have, could you?
Susan (*considering*) Oh yes, I could. I'm stronger than I look, you know.
Briers That's not what I meant.
Susan What did you mean?
Briers Merely that if Mister was with you, then you must have been with him. If you're his alibi, he's yours.
Susan Do I need an alibi?
Briers They're always useful.
Susan (*to Humphrey*) Have you got one?
Humphrey No.
Susan Tut-tut. Well, thanks for telling me about mine. (*She stands up*) If there's anything I can do for you—either of you—any time . . . *Ciao.*

She sails out

Humphrey (*at length*) A remarkable offer.
Briers From a really dedicated little liar.
Humphrey You think she's lying?
Briers In detail and in depth. (*He coughs. At length, suddenly hard*) And you don't always come clean, either, do you Humphrey?

Humphrey waits

You didn't mention that Loseby liked boys as well as girls.
Humphrey (*after a pause*) Is it relevant?
Briers Vital. He's completely changed his story. First it was a girl he was in bed with that night. Now it's a young man.
Humphrey Did he specify?
Briers A brother officer.
Humphrey Nothing like keeping it in the regiment.
Briers When I told him we'd checked with his club and he hadn't spent the weekend there he produced the chap—his name is Gimson—who duly confirmed this latest version of events.
Humphrey They could both be lying.
Briers Oh yes, everybody could be lying about everything and no doubt almost everybody is. But he seemed genuinely fond of Loseby. And even in this enlightened age most of us would be unlikely to invent that particular sophistication.
Humphrey Loseby's a cool customer.
Briers Also, at times, a violent one. But I can't for the life of me see why he should want to murder the old lady. Or why anyone else should want to. There seems to be no motive.
Humphrey Oh, come . . .
Briers Can you suggest one?
Humphrey Several.

Briers For example?

Humphrey Sex? Old women have been raped before.

Briers Not a vestige of a sign.

Humphrey Money?

Briers None of you would kill for a few hundred pounds in notes.

Humphrey There could be more, stashed away.

Briers We've turned the house inside out.

Humphrey A beneficiary under the Will?

Briers None of you benefits substantially. I'm not supposed to tell you that. I hope it's not a disappointment. There's no one with a conceivable motive. With one exception.

Humphrey Who is that?

Briers You.

Humphrey (*at length*) That's an interesting flight of fancy.

Briers Not fancy. Fact. You're the only one we've got a motive for.

Pause

Humphrey May I hear it?

Briers It's political.

Humphrey I'm fascinated.

Briers So was I, when I learnt that when you were up at Cambridge you were an "Apostle".

Pause

Humphrey Who dug that up?

Briers Norman.

Humphrey Who's Norman?

Briers Inspector Shingler. Is it true?

Pause

Humphrey Yes. But, if I may, to coin a phrase, put it *bluntly*, not every member of that exclusive Cambridge dining club was a Soviet agent — at the time or subsequently.

Briers Quite. But if you were one of those who was — if you continued to be after you came down — if you still *are*, and Lady Ashbrook knew and was holding it over you . . .

Humphrey Assuming there was anything to hold — how would she know?

Briers Through her husband. Whitehall talks to Whitehall's wives and at the time of the Burgess and MacLean affair you were investigated — (*tapping Shingler's paper*) — it's all here, neatly documented — investigated three times.

Humphrey And three times cleared of any connection whatsoever.

Briers In common with others who were later proved to be traitors.

Pause

Humphrey (*stung, but still just under control*) He should go a long way, your Inspector Shingler.

Briers Was it you?

Humphrey You haven't cautioned me.
Briers *Was it you?*

Pause

Humphrey No. But then, as Miss Rice-Davies would say, I would say that wouldn't I?
Briers (*getting up*) For God's sake, man! (*After a pause*) Murder happened in this room. There's someone moving about, going through the normal workaday routine which one takes as unthinkingly as breathing. I don't know what's driving him, but I'm going to find him, because I want that person more than I've ever wanted anything in my life. (*He moves to the portrait*)
Humphrey What's driving *you?*
Briers (*gradually*) She sprang from an England that was very different from the present. The England of my youth. We said "England" then, not "Britain", or "United Kingdom", though that was what we meant, and no Scot, no Irishman or Welshman took offence. Somehow "England" warmed and embraced us all . . . I have an unreasoning, an almost neurotic regard for that period and that memory. . . . We no longer have an Empire. We're no longer the workshop of the world. We even have a problem paying our way. But until quite recently this was still a land of tolerance and gentleness. Now that, too, is disappearing like a dream. . . . Whoever it was will be smoked out—*smoked out* and brought to justice. (*To the portrait*) You have my word.

Briers stares up at the portrait like a priest before an altar as—

the CURTAIN *falls*

ACT II

SCENE 1

The same. A few days later

The numbers on the blackboard, denoting the visits by detectives to houses in the South London area, have risen. Otherwise the room, like the weather, remains the same

When the CURTAIN *rises Briers is in his shirt sleeves at the trestle table speaking on the telephone. Shingler is seated at the small desk upstage, typing*

Briers Yes, sir, that's the score up to last night. For what it's worth, we've covered half London. . . . It may be useful, Commissioner, but it's small stuff, chicken feed, and it's not leading anywhere. . . . I still think so, sir. The key is here in this house. . . . *Instinct*, Commissioner. . . . Yes, sir, I'm getting impatient too. (*He hangs up and coughs*) Which reminds me. How long have we kept her waiting?

Shingler An hour.

Briers That should cool her heels, if no other part of her anatomy. Wheel her in, Norman.

Shingler You think she'll talk?

Briers She'll talk all right. Whether she'll talk anything like the truth is something else again.

Shingler goes and opens the door

Shingler (*motioning to someone off*) Come in.

Susan enters, escorted by a uniformed Policewoman who comes in and closes the door behind them. The Policewoman remains by the door

Susan looks delectably unruffled. She is carrying a multi-coloured shoulder bag. Briers ignores her and busies himself at the trestle table

Susan (*to Shingler*) Hi. (*To Briers*) Hello.

Briers (*curtly, without looking up*) Sit down, sit down.

Susan I know. (*Indicating the sofa*) Not there. Here. (*She plonks herself happily in the winged armchair and crosses her legs*) I'm beginning to feel quite at home.

Shingler goes and sits on the sofa and takes out his notebook

Briers (*abruptly*) Do you like gardens?

Susan Gardens?

Briers Yes. Those open spaces where things grow — if the soil is cultivated.

Susan You're in a funny mood.

Briers Mine is becoming seriously neglected. What's more it's likely to stay neglected unless you stop wasting my time.

Susan Listen, *you're* the one who keeps sending for *me*. Just for the record I was here on the dot and you're an hour late.

Briers Miss Thirkill, you see those flats at the bottom of the garden, the ones facing the mews?

Susan Uh-huh.

Briers A couple living there have just told us that on the night Lady Ashbrook was done to death there was a girl hanging about the mews when they went out to dinner. That was about eight-thirty on the Saturday night. When they came back, somewhere between ten-thirty and eleven, the girl was still there, walking about between the mews and the street. They gave us a description of the girl. (*He glances at Shingler*)

Shingler (*reading from his notebook*) Light brown hair, medium height, smartish clothes, trousers, carrying a multi-coloured shoulder bag.

Susan calmly slips her multi-coloured shoulder bag off her shoulder, opens it and proceeds to apply lipstick

Susan (*between applications*) Of course you realize . . . that could be . . . just about anybody north . . . or, for that matter, south . . . of the Mason-Dixon line?

Briers Technically it could be just about anybody, yes. But in fact it wasn't, was it? It was you.

Susan (*laughing*) Me? For heaven's sakes, how could it be me? I was with Mister practically the whole weekend. I told you.

Briers In considerable detail.

Susan Well then. I couldn't be with Mister and walking about the mews at the same time, could I?

Briers We managed to work that out.

Shingler You lied to us, miss.

Susan That's not a very nice thing to say.

Briers Miss Thirkill, you've concocted an entirely bogus story about where you were and who you were with that night. You've gone further. You've signed a written statement, confirming it. That's a serious offence. Don't you think you'd better consider your position?

Susan I've told you, I was with Mister and he was with me.

Briers (*with rising impatience*) No, he wasn't. He was not with you. We've known for some time who he was with and why.

Susan Who was he with and why?

Briers It doesn't matter. We're satisfied about his movements. That's all you need to know.

Susan (*after a pause*) All right. I lied. I was only trying to keep Mister's nose clean. He was with Duggie Gimson. They were being all boys together, weren't they? Not for the first time. . . . Mister's such an ass. He's not really gay, you know. Not that it would matter if he was, live and let live. And he's not ambidextrous either. It's just a game with him, variety the spice and so forth. All the same, I must have a little talk with Mister.

Briers Do. By all means have a little talk with Mister. Meanwhile, perhaps you'd be so good as to have a little talk with us and, if it wouldn't be too much trouble, tell us where the hell you were that night? (*He takes a swig of medicine*)

Susan (*carefully*) I'll tell you this. If it *was* me in the mews — and I'm not saying it was, I'm not saying it wasn't — but if I was there, waiting about for hours, I couldn't have been in here murdering the old girl, could I?

Briers We managed to work that out, too.

Susan Then why am I here?

Shingler You're helping the police with their enquiries, miss.

Susan For the nth time.

Shingler If you'd rather not, there's no compulsion.

Susan (*to Briers*) Listen, I'm on your side.

Briers I'm not sure whether that makes me feel better or worse.

Susan I do care for you, really I do.

Briers In that case where were you that night, Miss Thirkill, and what the devil were you up to?

No reply

Miss Thirkill?

Susan I wish you'd call me Susan. Well now, let me think. It was a very hot night. And I had no-one to take me out. I think — I'm not certain, mind, but I *think* I went for a long walk. Yes, I'm sure I did. No, I didn't. Or did I? . . . I say, are you feeling all right?

Briers As well as can be expected in the circumstances.

Susan Shall I press on regardless?

Briers Yes, yes, yes. Continue.

Susan (*suddenly*) Eureka! Got it! Saturday night! Of course! Now we're getting somewhere.

Briers I do most prayerfully and profoundly hope so.

Susan *Faites attention*. There's no-one in the flats so I ring around to see if any of my chums is home. No dice. Everybody out of town. The heat. I begin to feel more and more at a loose end. So I decide to call up Mister in Germany. Surprise, surprise. The Duty Officer says he's most frightfully sorry but Mister's on compassionate leave. His grandmother, failing fast. So I go rushing round here.

Briers (*sharply*) Then you *were* in this house, this room, that night?

Susan I'm telling you.

Briers (*wearily*) You've told me so many things, Miss Thirkill.

Susan (*indignantly*) But this one's true. For heaven's sakes, don't you want to hear the truth from me?

Briers Never having had that experience, I couldn't say. All right, all right. What time?

Susan What time what?

Briers What time did you arrive here?

Susan A little after eight. Say ten past.

Briers What happened?

Susan No sign of Mister and Grandma chirpy as a sparrow. I guess in a flash what he's up to and who with but I don't want to get him in schtuck with his granny so I let it go. We make conversation for a minute or two. The radio is on. Some waltz or other. Strauss, I think. It takes her back to ten sixty-six or whenever she was young. She even dances a few steps. Well, it's not exactly Hot Gossip, but I've seen worse at *Annabel's*.

Briers Miss Thirkill, are you making all this up?

Susan Would I do that to you?

Briers nods to Shingler to take over the interrogation

Shingler (*getting up and going* DR *of Susan*) How long were you here?

Susan Three, four minutes at the most.

Shingler And then?

Susan I say "nighty-night, sleep tight" and I'm on my way.

Shingler (*hard, fast*) So you left the house but you didn't leave the area? You hung around the mews?

Susan I might have done.

Shingler Yes or no? Was it you in the mews that night or wasn't it?

Susan (*to Briers*) Are you going to let him bully me?

Briers Answer the question.

Susan It was me, it was me, it was me. There.

Shingler You hung around on the off chance that he might come home? Right?

Susan On the off chance that *who* might come home?

Shingler Captain Loseby.

Susan Wrong.

Shingler Who, then? Who *were* you waiting for?

The intercom buzzes

Briers (*answering the intercom*) Yes? . . . Ask him to wait.

Shingler I said, who were you waiting for?

Susan Toby.

Shingler (*from one side of her*) Toby Who?

Susan Toby Bennett.

Briers (*going to the other side of her*) Who is Toby Bennett?

Susan One of my ex-es. He has a flat in the mews. I used to borrow it from time to time.

Shingler What for?

Susan It wasn't always convenient to take a boy back to my place.

Briers Why?

Susan (*head swivelling from one to the other*) I wish you'd make up your mind who's serving. Because when Mummy or Daddy were in town they used it as a pied-à-terre.

Briers And were Mummy or Daddy in town that night?

Susan No.

Shingler Would you like a lawyer, miss?

Susan Whatever for? Look, I was mad at Mister and I had a sudden yen to see Toby again. But when he's working he doesn't get home until the small hours. He plays a synthesizer in a disco. So I waited.

Briers And when he'd finished playing his synthesizer did he turn up?
Susan No. He was up to here at Hammersmith with Samantha. But I didn't know that, did I?
Shingler How long did you wait out there?
Susan Till about four.
Briers (*incredulously*) Nearly eight hours?
Susan When I really want something, I can wait for it. Finally I gave up and went and had a coffee at the all-night stall at Hyde Park Corner.
Briers And between approximately eight-thirty p.m. and four a.m. did you see anyone enter or leave this house?
Susan Not a soul, unless they came down the chimney.
Shingler Look, miss. You can't have stood in one place with a view of two doors to the house for eight whole hours without moving.
Susan I didn't say I didn't move. Of course I moved, I walked up and down, up and down—all I needed was a poodle. But if anyone had gone in or out of here I'd have known. You don't believe me.
Briers Not without reason.

Loseby strides forcefully in with Sergeant Tanner at his heels

Loseby (*turning on Tanner; belligerantly*) You want to try another round?
Tanner Sorry, sir. He——
Susan (*getting up and going to Loseby*) Hello, darling. Had a good day?

Tanner goes and stands with the Policewoman who now stands with her back against the door

Loseby (*to Briers*) If you've been putting Susie through the wringer——

Briers sits in his chair

Susan No, no. They've been absolutely sweet. (*To Briers*) He's so protective. I've been telling them our news, darling, and how you're going to make the best husband a girl ever had.
Briers (*sharply*) Husband?
Susan Didn't I get around to it? I was just about to.
Briers (*to Loseby*) You're married?
Loseby No. Engaged.

Susan holds up her left hand, flashing a diamond ring. Pause

Briers Congratulations

Shingler mumbles something unintelligible, if not unprintable

Susan Thank you. Everyone's delighted, aren't they, darling? Especially Mummy and Daddy. They worry about me.
Briers (*softly*) One can understand.
Loseby (*loudly*) What does that mean?
Susan (*going to the winged armchair and picking up her bag*) We have our eye on a rented house in Radnor Walk. We're hoping to buy, aren't we, darling, when Mister gets his next little instalment from the Comptroller? Well, if you're all through with me——

Briers (*sharply*) What did you say?

Susan If there's nothing more you want to ask me——

Briers You mentioned the Comptroller.

Susan Did I? I expect I was just . . . fantasizing.

Briers No, you weren't. You were talking clearly and convincingly for once. We're already interested in that operation. Who and what is the Comptroller?

Loseby A family joke.

Susan A name for money coming out of the blue.

Loseby Providence.

Susan God.

Loseby The Comptroller.

Susan It's a name Mister used to call his grandmother when she gave him a large tip.

Shingler You're lying again.

Briers Who is the Comptroller?

Loseby I haven't a notion.

Briers You're saying that money reaches you and you don't know under heaven where it comes from?

Loseby Exactly.

Briers You expect me to believe that?

Loseby (*loudly*) I don't give a damn whether you believe it or not.

Briers rises

Briers (*furiously*) Of course you know where it comes from—or if you don't, you can make an educated guess.

Loseby It must come somehow from my grandmother. That's all I know.

Susan And I don't even know that much—which suits me nicely. I don't think a girl ought to be too inquisitive about her husband's source of income. I don't think it's a wife's place, do you? (*To Loseby, firmly*) Come along, Lozenge, we're leaving.

She leads Loseby to the door

(*To the Policewoman*) Excuse me.

Briers nods. The Policewoman and Tanner step aside

Thank you so much.

Susan and Loseby exit. Susan re-enters at once

(*To Briers*) We'll send you an invitation to the wedding. I do hope you'll come. (*To Shingler*) Both of you. (*To Tanner*) All of you.

She sails out, Tanner and the Policewoman in train

Briers Christ, I'd rather have half a dozen teeth out. You know, she doesn't even lie for a purpose. She just does it for the sheer bloody beauty of it.

Shingler Wedding bells! I give it a month.

Briers There, oddly enough, you could be wrong, Norman. Today's impossibles often turn out to be tomorrow's solid citizens.

Shingler Not Thirkill. She'll be in and out of her four-poster with Tom, Dick and Harry before the honeymoon's a day——

Briers Shut up. Shut up. (*Holding up his hand for silence; with growing excitement*) She was waiting in the mews from eight-thirty until about four o'clock the following morning, and when I asked her whether, in all that time, anybody went in or out of the house, she said not a soul.

Shingler She can't possibly know that for certain.

Briers *But suppose it's true?* (*He buzzes the intercom*) Send in Colonel Leigh. (*To Shingler*) And, Norman, I want him alone.

Shingler Is that a very good idea, sir?

Briers *Alone.*

Shingler goes out

Humphrey enters and goes to the winged armchair

Briers goes to the french windows. Pause

Humphrey I realize I'm no longer *persona grata.*

Briers (*turning to him*) I thought you'd like to know that I know the way it was done.

Humphrey You know how?

Briers Oh yes.

Humphrey And who?

Briers It's narrowing down.

Pause

Humphrey You're getting close?

Briers Very.

Humphrey Do you want to tell me?

Briers (*suddenly*) No, you tell me. What am I looking for?

Pause

Humphrey (*gradually*) You're looking for a man who knows how to keep his cool under pressure. A man out of the common rut.

Briers Yes. (*He moves about the room, circling Humphrey*)

Humphrey Not a professional villain, but a man professionally trained. Someone to whom death, even violent death, is no stranger . . .

Briers Go on.

Humphrey There are three candidates. If Loseby is ruled out——

Briers He's out.

Humphrey You're left with two, of whom I am obviously one. Counter-productive to remind you it was I who asked for your assignment to this case. As you rightly pointed out, I never could resist a challenge and, if I'm the man you're looking for, such a challenge could be irresistible. (*He sits in the winged armchair*) Also, if that young protégé of yours, damn his fertile, probing mind, is to be believed, I could have a motive, however convoluted and bizarre. Am I reading you?

Briers With precision. (*He goes to the trestle table*)

Humphrey I may or may not have murdered Cousin Madge, the fact that I deny it is to be expected. In your shoes I'd keep an open mind.

Briers My mind is open.

Humphrey You'd disappoint me if it wasn't. In which case you're left with a choice between me and the only other possibility. Either way you're also left with the trifling inconvenience of having to make it stick in law with the evidence available. If, as I suspect, it's thin, bloody thin, you'll have to break him, won't you, whichever of us it is? You're rather good at that, as I recall. If he doesn't break, there's not a great deal you can do about it, is there? (*He rises and turns to go*)

Briers (*hard*) Sit down, Humphrey.

Pause. Humphrey sits. They face each other

The Lights fade to Black-out

SCENE 2

The same. Autumn, early evening

The drawing-room is all but back to normal with the blackboard, filing cabinets, noticeboard and all the paraphernalia of external investigations removed. Only a few papers remain on the writing-desk. The french windows are closed and the alcove curtains once again open

As the Lights come up Briers paces, expectant. He coughs, glances at his watch, goes to the writing-desk, pours some cough mixture and drinks

Shingler enters

Shingler He's here.

Briers Right.

Shingler starts out

And, Norman — exactly as we planned it. When I throw you out, not far, outside the door, no further.

Shingler Understood.

Shingler exits, leaving the door open

Briers sits at the writing-desk, picks up some papers and becomes seemingly immersed

(*Off*) I think you know the way.

Dr Perryman (*off*) Yes, indeed.

Dr Perryman is shown in by Shingler, who follows, closing the door behind them. Shingler remains upstage

Briers Good-afternoon, Doctor.

Dr Perryman Good-evening, Chief Superintendent. (*Looking round the room*) Almost back to normal. Coming to the end of your investigation?

Briers There are still one or two things we'd like to clear up. I'm sorry to bother you again. We thought perhaps you might be able to help us further.

Dr Perryman I doubt that, but I'll do my best.

Briers I'm sure you will, I won't keep you a moment.

Shingler Sit down, sir.

Dr Perryman sits on the sofa. Briers works at the desk

A Stenographer enters, carrying a notebook and pencil, and sits at the whatnot table

Dr Perryman registers the presence of the Stenographer without concern

Briers (*finally turning to Dr Perryman*) Why don't we start with Lady Ashbrook's standard of living? It's something of a puzzle.

Dr Perryman In what way precisely?

Briers (*going to the* DL *chair*) How she managed to live like this on her income. That is, on the income she returned to the Revenue. You see, she had a trifle from investments in this country, an annuity of fifteen hundred pounds and her old-age pension. Out of that she had to pay rates, heating, lighting and the daily woman. She was not extravagant but she still bought good clothes, and a smart hairdresser came to the house once a week. The question is, where did the money come from?

Dr Perryman I know nothing of any details. As her doctor I often advised her to have someone permanently in the house but she always said she couldn't afford it.

Briers On the face of it she was right. We couldn't make out how she managed financially. Especially after her Will — her very modest Will — was published. You see, Doctor, her day-to-day expenses, her apparently limited means — they simply didn't balance out. Until we managed, that is, to unearth the truth about the American fund.

Dr Perryman The American fund?

Briers You know, Doctor. The Comptroller fund. That's how she paid her bills. With money that came over from the States at regular intervals.

Dr Perryman American money?

Briers No. English currency. It was sent across in cash to a poste restante.

Dr Perryman That's most interesting. And of course it would explain the discrepancy between her way of life and the apparent lack of means to support it.

Briers It would. It does.

Dr Perryman This one-way traffic — has it continued after her death?

Briers Oh yes. A sizeable sum has been passed to her grandson. Our information is, passed by you, Doctor.

Dr Perryman (*amused*) By me?

The Policewoman enters with two mugs of tea on a tray which she puts on the sofa table

Briers We believe you were also responsible for passing money from the fund to Lady Ashbrook in her lifetime. (*He goes and sits next to Dr Perryman on the sofa*) Oh, thank you, Ann.

The Policewoman exits

Sugar?

Dr Perryman Thank you, no.

Briers sets a mug of tea in front of him

Briers Yes, you were the Comptroller, weren't you, Doctor?

Dr Perryman The What?

Briers The Comptroller. C-O-M-P-T-R-O-L-L-E-R. As in "Comptroller of the Royal Household". The word must have appealed to the old lady's social instincts. (*He coughs*)

Dr Perryman Forgive me, that cough of yours—how long have you had it?

Briers As long as I've had this job.

Dr Perryman You must be under a lot of strain.

Briers No more than you.

Dr Perryman I can't say I'm ever conscious of being under pressure.

Briers Then you're an even more unusual man than I take you to be. (*He coughs again*)

Dr Perryman If I were your doctor, I should want to have those lungs of yours examined. Regularly.

Briers But you're not my doctor, are you, Doctor? Yes, we know that you passed money to the old lady during her lifetime, and after her death to others. We know the money came from a firm of lawyers in New York, one of whom had been an intimate friend of your patient's in her younger days. We believe that when the money arrived here, it was collected by you— Lady Ashbrook being at first too conspicuous and ultimately too old to do so herself. An ingenious method of avoiding tax while she was alive and death duties when she wasn't. The money was in fact interest from her late husband's American securities, plus slices of capital which was being allowed to decline. Shall I go on?

Dr Perryman (*after a pause, with a broad smile*) It was a benevolent service, done to help an old friend, old in every sense, to end her days in something approaching the manner to which she was accustomed.

Briers We'll leave the benevolence or otherwise to the Inland Revenue. It was certainly an ingenious scheme, dependent on a reliable courier, a role for which you were admirably suited.

Dr Perryman She had been my patient for many years.

Briers And she trusted you.

Dr Perryman Yes.

Briers In the event of her death did she tell you what to do?

Dr Perryman She did.

Briers Who was to benefit?

Dr Perryman Her grandson, chiefly. One or two others. The sums were small, with one exception. Loseby was to get twenty thousand pounds.

Shingler And you've done all this for nothing?

Dr Perryman No. I'm her executor. I'm to take a commission from what's left of the estate. It can hardly be substantial. The lease of this house has only eighteen months to run.

Briers (*abruptly*) All right. Now let's drop all this. We shouldn't be spending our time on a minor piece of tax evasion.

Dr Perryman What should we be spending our time on?

Briers Murder. It's the murder we want to ask you about, Doctor.

Dr Perryman By all means.

Briers You were in this house the night Lady Ashbrook died.

Dr Perryman As I told you, for approximately half an hour.

Briers Uninvited. On your own initiative.

Dr Perryman Am I to be charged with breaking and entering?

Briers No. You didn't break in, Doctor. Three people beside the old lady, had a key. The daily woman, who was at a Spanish party that particular night; her grandson, who was holding a rather more individual party of his own; and you. You had your own front door key, Doctor.

Dr Perryman Naturally. I was her physician. She was old. I had to be able to enter in an emergency.

Briers Being her physician put you in a special category, didn't it?

Dr Perryman I'm not sure that I follow you.

Briers If it's a question of killing an old lady, her doctor has certain advantages. She's used to him. She's used to his hands.

Dr Perryman examines his hands

You have good hands, Doctor. Sensitive hands. A surgeon's hands.

Dr Perryman It happens to be my profession.

Briers And there'd be other advantages. You'd know exactly where to put those hands. And there'd be no fingerprints. A doctor would have surgical gloves readily available.

Dr Perryman (*highly entertained*) If you should take to murder, Chief Superintendent, society had better watch out.

Briers There's just one thing we still don't understand.

Dr Perryman Only one?

Briers Why smash her skull in? Was it in a fit of madness or the final touch in your attempt to make it look like the work of a thief, a professional villain who broke in and went berserk? The garden door forced—with a scalpel, was it?—the silver dishes stolen from the dining-room—the controlled mayhem in this room—by the way, a little too controlled—you should have left the desk drawer open, villains don't tidy up after them.

Dr Perryman You really have a most remarkable imagination.

Briers Let me take it a stage further. . . . Let's imagine a man with a good— no, the highest possible opinion of himself—wanting to do something on a grand scale. A man who knows he's ten times brighter than the rest of us. Surrounded all his life by dull brutes, cattle. And cool. A man who doesn't break under stress, who can take the ultimate horrors in his stride. The sort of man who could have run Belsen or Buchenwald without flinching. Can you imagine such a man, Doctor?

Dr Perryman Not as well as you can.

Briers Oh, I couldn't feel like that. But I can imagine someone who did
saying to himself: "There's no limit to me, to my capacity. And I'll prove it,
above all to myself." Of course he'd have one weakness that he'd need to
guard against. He'd have to be the vainest man you'd ever met.

Dr Perryman glances at his watch and rises

Dr Perryman Chief Superintendent, I do have a number of patients——
Briers (*suddenly hard, brutal*) Sit down, Doctor.

Dr Perryman sits again

In the summer you thought that the old lady was about to die.
Dr Perryman My clinical judgement was that it was rather more probable
than not.
Briers But your clinical judgement turned out to be wrong?
Dr Perryman It happens to the best of us.
Briers If your judgement had been right, Lady Ashbrook would have been
dead by now from natural causes? And you would have been dealing with
her financial arrangements just as you are at present?
Dr Perryman Yes.
Briers And as there had been no murder no-one would have thought twice
about it. The money would have continued to come in according to plan?
Dr Perryman Naturally.
Briers But since your judgement didn't prove right she might have lived for
years?
Dr Perryman She could have done.
Briers It must have been a massive shock to learn that she was going to
survive.
Dr Perryman It was a profound relief.
Briers Was it? She was old. She had grown increasingly demanding. She
must frequently have been a drain on your energies, as the old inevitably
are. Not the easiest of human beings, no doubt maddening at times. . . . The
prospect of going on when you had thought your release was coming.
When you had got used to the idea. The temptation to put an end to it when
nature unexpectedly declined to oblige ... was that the moment of
decision, Doctor?
Dr Perryman (*rising; suddenly*) I should like to make a statement.

Swiftly Shingler opens his notebook, pen poised

No, not that kind of statement, Inspector. (*To Briers*) I have work to do.
This is a serious interference. It might be more than that for some of my
patients. If you continue to detain me, I shall be obliged to ask for legal
advice.
Briers (*indicating the telephone*) Please, if you wish, call your solicitor.

Dr Perryman glances at the telephone, hesitates and finally makes no move

In that case—(*with growing pace and force*)—you believed your patient's
hospital tests would be positive?
Dr Perryman I thought it possible.

Shingler (*in a flash*) "Probable". You said "probable".

Shingler glances at the Stenographer who checks the shorthand notes

Stenographer (*reading in a flat voice*) "My clinical judgement was that it was rather more probable than not."

Dr Perryman (*very slightly nettled*) All right, all right, "probable".

Briers Your patient believed she might be terminally ill?

Dr Perryman We both believed it.

Briers Did she talk about her death?

Dr Perryman She didn't pretend.

Briers If the worst came to the worst, you could ease her out quietly. Did she talk about that?

Dr Perryman I'm not prepared to reveal a conversation between doctor and patient. (*He sits again*)

Briers Then there was one?

Dr Perryman I haven't said so. She appeared to be in an extreme situation. Then she heard the news from the laboratory. The extreme situation ceased to exist.

Briers And her dependence on you — for release if necessary — ceased with it?

Dr Perryman I was still her doctor.

Shingler (*loud, hard*) You were a helluva lot more than that, weren't you? It isn't every doctor manages his patient's money.

Dr Perryman (*to Briers*) I thought we'd finished with that business.

Shingler (*moving nearer to Dr Perryman; crescendo*) If she died of natural causes you would have been in control of the American fund. When you realized she wasn't under threat of death, was that when you decided "forget about euthanasia, I'm going to cave the old bitch's head in"?

Dr Perryman (*springing to his feet*) This is outrageous!

Briers (*with cold fury*) Brutal murders are an outrage — to society, to decency, to ordinary human feeling. They degrade and debase those who commit them, and if we're not bloody careful they do the same to us who try to bring the murderers to justice. *Sit down, Doctor.*

Momentarily shaken by this outburst, Dr Perryman obeys

Dr Perryman (*with total calm*) You're a violent man, Chief Superintendent. You have violence in you.

Briers controls himself with an effort

Shingler The American fund — you realize we have the facts?

Dr Perryman I'm not prepared to answer questions from this officer.

Shingler Why? Because you're scared? Scared to bloody death? Scared you'd incriminate yourself? Why else would you refuse to talk? Eh?

Briers (*softly*) Norman. (*He indicates to Shingler to go out*)

Shingler exits

Briers gets up and gives the tea tray to the Stenographer

The Stenographer exits, closing the door behind her

Briers goes to the writing-desk and takes a dose of medicine

Dr Perryman A palliative, I'm afraid, not a cure.

Briers *(ignoring this; at length)* You . . . are an exceptional man, Doctor. And you know it, you've always known it. Oh, you conceal it brilliantly under a diffident, almost commonplace manner. But you're not a commonplace person.

Dr Perryman goes to the winged armchair DR *and sits*

You're not like ordinary men, who obey the ordinary human rules.

Dr Perryman What are the ordinary human rules?

Briers If you don't know them, that would be interesting. But of course you do. The real point, for a man like you, is what makes people keep them.

Dr Perryman I think I know that. Do you?

Briers It used to be religion. Fear of judgement in the after life. Today? Fear of what other people think, that's still there, of course. But mostly it's fear of the law. Without the law there wouldn't be much left. The trouble is, Doctor, you are without fear. You don't fear the law. You don't fear anything. Behind the gentle, civilized façade of a ministering physician, there's a totally fearless man.

Dr Perryman An unexpected testimonial.

Briers Do you accept it?

Dr Perryman I accept that it's fear that makes most of us conform. If there weren't fear, how would everyone behave?

Briers Horribly. No, not everyone. But enough to make the world a shambles.

Dr Perryman You'd rather they conformed like good tame beasts?

Briers Of course I would—and so would any sane person. . . . Why did you kill her, Doctor? It can't just have been the money. There wasn't enough to motivate a doctor with a successful practice. Were you testing yourself to the limit? Or was it—yes, was it that after a lifetime of caring for people, the desire to break with the past, to turn your world upside down, to *destroy*, became on a sudden overwhelming? Like a priest, whose life has been given to God, finding himself irresistibly drawn to the Devil . . .?

Dr Perryman is totally impassive

(Moving upstage of the DL *chair)* Let me tell you what I think you did. Let's go back to that Saturday night . . .

During the following, the Lights fade slowly to just a single spot on Briers. The scene that follows should have a certain gauze-like quality in style and lighting

(Quietly, gradually) You didn't call here in the early evening as you said in your statement. Susan Thirkill was prowling the mews for hours, on the watch for someone else. She didn't see a glimpse of anyone coming in or going out. Not the slightest sign. You must have been here from the middle or late afternoon until the small hours.

From the darkened section of the stage Dr Perryman exits through the alcove as Lady Ashbrook enters and sits in the winged armchair

We think you waited, unseen, upstairs in a bedroom. It must have been a shock when you heard the bell ring about eight and Susan Thirkill coming up the stairs. But she went away. Had she stayed. . . . Still you waited, while the shadows lengthened on the lawn, while you psyched yourself up for what you had to do . . .

Fade to Black-out

and then at last, when you were ready in your mind, you came quietly . . . very quietly . . . down the stairs . . .

Briers exits through the downstage french window

The drawing-room is now as it was the previous summer, but seen as though through a glass darkly. It is after nine p.m. and the room is full of shadows. The french windows are open to the garden

The Lights come up on Lady Ashbrook, sitting in the winged armchair in a single pool of light from the lamp on the whatnot table. On the small table beside her is a tray with the remains of a light meal. She is listening to a record player, reasonably modern, but by no means the latest model, which is on a small table on her other side. It is playing a lush recording of Strauss's "Emperor Waltz" and the rich romantic music fills the night air

Behind her, part of the upstage wall becomes transparent, revealing a dimly lit part of the landing and the stairs to the upper floor

Dr Perryman appears on the stairs, carrying his medical bag. He comes very quietly down the stairs to the landing

Suddenly, the old lady hears a slight noise from outside the room. She turns the music down

Lady Ashbrook (*sharply*) Who's that? Who's there?

No reply. She switches the music off

Is someone there?

The door opens and Dr Perryman stands in the doorway

(*With relief*) Oh, it's you, Ralph. I didn't hear the front door.
Dr Perryman Did I alarm you?
Lady Ashbrook I'm not easily alarmed. But there are those who are, you should make more noise when entering a house. Come in, come in.

He comes in, closing the door softly behind him. The Lights on the landing fade and the wall becomes once more opaque.

Dr Perryman I hope I'm not disturbing you.
Lady Ashbrook Yes, but it doesn't matter. I was just playing the *Kaiserwaltzer* on the gramophone. I refuse to say "record player". Such a functional expression. A particularly fine performance by the Vienna Philharmonic. You're familiar with it, of course.
Dr Perryman I don't think so.

Lady Ashbrook You don't know what you're missing. Only the Viennese know how to play Johann Strauss. Richard is another matter. At once more difficult and much easier.

Dr Perryman puts his bag behind the sofa and goes to the drinks table

Help yourself—or do you still have calls to make?
Dr Perryman You're my last.
Lady Ashbrook Oh? I didn't send for you. Is this an official visit?
Dr Perryman No.
Lady Ashbrook That's all right, then. I'm always pleased to see you, but less so when I'm paying for the pleasure.

Dr Perryman helps himself to a large brandy

Dr Perryman What will *you* have?
Lady Ashbrook Nothing. I've only just had supper. Maria left me what she calls one of her Spanish specials. I can only say if that's what passes for cuisine in Spain, no wonder the Basques are in revolt. Not that I'm hungry in this heat.
Dr Perryman (*going to the french windows*) It's cooler as the darkness closes in.
Lady Ashborok I don't particularly care for the darkness.
Dr Perryman Really? I rather like it. (*He scans the garden while taking care not to be seen doing so*) But I'm interrupting your music.
Lady Ashbrook Oh, music is company. Like smoking. And for some reason I felt nervy tonight. But I don't need it now you're here. (*She examines the needle of the record player*) Oh bother!
Dr Perryman (*putting his glass down*) There should always be someone here, Madge. In times like these you should have a housekeeper or companion living in.
Lady Ashbrook So you've said repeatedly. I can't afford it. (*She fiddles with the record player*) Pass me the toolbox under the desk, this wretched pick-up is always coming loose.

Dr Perryman takes the toolbox to her

Dr Perryman Buy a new machine.
Lady Ashbrook I can't afford that either. There's a small screwdriver here somewhere. (*She takes a hammer out and puts it on her lap, rifles through the contents of the box, finds a screwdriver and fiddles with the pick-up arm*) It's curious. When I was young I was hopeless with my hands, but in my old age, do you know, I'm quite a whizz at do-it-yourself. There, that should fix it. (*She replaces the tools and re-starts the record player*)

Dr Perryman puts the toolbox back beneath the desk. For a moment the "Emperor Waltz" fills the room then she turns it off

There. That's it. You know, if one had a choice when to be alive, Vienna in her heyday would be mine. Doesn't that strike you as the perfect time?
Dr Perryman With no antibiotics? No penicillin? No sulphonamides?
Lady Ashbrook And no proper dentures. I know. They say the drains were

dreadful too. But oh, the music. That lives on. That's all that matters, to live on.

Dr Perryman (*producing a small bottle of pills from his pocket*) I brought you these.

Lady Ashbrook What are they?

Dr Perryman Vitamins. Here try a couple. (*He shakes two pills into his hand*)

Lady Ashbrook (*waving them away*) My dear man, I don't need pills, not now. Thanks to you. You gave me a whole new lease of life.

Dr Perryman I?

Lady Ashbrook When you insisted that I take those tests. The result, the lifting of the shadow, suddenly all was changed.

Dr Perryman Yes. . . . (*Proffering the pills again*) Can't I persuade you? It will be easier this way.

Lady Ashbrook Easier?

Dr Perryman To regain your health.

Lady Ashbrook But I've never felt better.

He replaces the pills in the bottle and the bottle in his pocket

What time do you make it?

Dr Perryman Nine-sixteen.

Lady Ashbrook That's all right, then. We've still got a few minutes.

Dr Perryman (*sharply*) For what?

Lady Ashbrook I've got a date. Directly after the News.

Dr Perryman A date? Here?

Lady Ashbrook Certainly. (*She sings*) "I danced with a man, who danced with a girl, who danced with the Prince of Wales." Don't look so alarmed. They're doing a re-run of the *Edward and Mrs Simpson* serial on television. I never miss it. I danced with that handsome creature on more than one occasion. He was a charmer if ever there was one.

Dr Perryman goes to the drinks table

And so were you, Ralph. So were you.

A nightingale in the summer night is heard

Listen. Nightingales aren't confined to Berkeley Square.

He pours himself another brandy

I've never known you take more than one before.

Dr Perryman It's been a difficult day. I lost a patient. A simple gastrectomy.

Lady Ashbrook Oh. I'm sorry.

Dr Perryman She came to just before the end. The look of astonishment on her face . . .

Lady Ashbrook Everyone lives with the certain prospect of death. No-one believes it will happen to *them*.

Dr Perryman One of the respects in which existence is merciful.

Lady Ashbrook Yes. . . . By the way, Ralph, I've made you my executor.

Dr Perryman Exec . . .

A Coat of Varnish

Lady Ashbrook Not that I aim to be troubling you for years. The way I feel
tonight I may well go for my century.
Dr Perryman (*returning his glass to the drinks table, suddenly active*) In that
case you won't want to catch cold. (*He closes the french windows*)
Lady Ashbrook In this heat? I like the air; what there is of it. Leave the
windows open, please.

He closes the curtains too

Ralph, did you hear what I said?
Dr Perryman Yes, I heard, but as your medical adviser I'm afraid I must
insist that you take proper care of yourself. Draughts can be dangerous.

*She watches him a moment, vaguely puzzled. He moves upstage of the sofa and
seems strangely excited*

Madge, did you know there's a statue of Newton in one of the Cambridge
colleges—Trinity, I think—with the inscription "*Qui genus humanum
ingenio superavit*—Who surpassed the entire human race with his genius".
Few of us can do that. But not to be part of the common herd . . . *that* we
can aspire to. That we can achieve . . . (*He pours a third brandy*)
Lady Ashbrook Ralph, I think you'd better go now and, if you're thinking of
driving——
Dr Perryman (*sitting on the arm of the sofa*) Did you ever drive, Madge? A
fast car? Really fast?
Lady Ashbrook Not myself. There was no lack of young men willing to drive
me as fast as I cared to go.
Dr Perryman (*eagerly*) And that was fast, wasn't it? Yes, you're that sort of
person. Were you ever scared?
Lady Ashbrook Not in the least.
Dr Perryman (*returning his glass to the drinks table*) No, you wouldn't be.
Fear has no more place in your make-up than it has in mine. I've just been
reading Rebecca West on the mind of murder. Fascinating. But I believe
she is wrong in one particular. "He who thinks of murder objectively is
dead in the most important part of him." Dead? No. Not dead. He who
thinks of murder objectively not only dares to drive the mind to the
brink—and over—he must surely be intensely, uniquely *alive*. (*He moves
swiftly over to the record player and puts the music on*) May we have the
music on?
Lady Ashbrook Ralph, you really are talking nonsense.
Dr Perryman Ssh. Quiet.
Lady Ashbrook I would like you to go now.
Dr Perryman (*in a world of his own*) No, Madge, no. Listen to the music.
Music for a nice pretty cushioned world. Music to escape reality.
Delightful—but deceptive. Civilization, Madge, is surface deep. There's
not much between us and our darker natures. Just about a coat of varnish
. . . (*His hands are at her throat*)

*She chokes almost soundlessly. He strangles her. The "Emperor Waltz" pours
into the room—fortissimo—deafening. Black-out*

Lady Ashbrook exits in the darkness

Dr Perryman sits in the winged armchair as before

Briers enters through the downstage french window and stands as before

The music fades and a spot comes up on Briers

Briers ... After you'd killed her—about nine-thirty, we think, no later than ten—you set about creating the impression of a burglary—the stolen money, the disordered room. ... Then you went downstairs ... you broke the lock of the garden door to distract attention from the front and still further strengthened the impression of an intruder ...

The Lights come up gradually on the drawing-room and Dr Perryman who still sits in the winged armchair

You removed some silver dishes from the dining-room to support the burglar theory and returned upstairs to hide them in your medical bag. You stayed here, here in the house of the woman you'd most brutally murdered, for several hours. Not many men could have done that. We think, without being certain, that you spent nearly all that time sitting quietly in her bedroom. We found a bit of fluff there from a suit of yours. The grey worsted.

Dr Perryman I must have worn that suit in that bedroom, forty, fifty times.

Briers Oh, it doesn't prove anything in itself. I just wanted you to know we're confident we know what happened. You worked out that we should wear ourselves into the ground, didn't you, trying to pick up sightings after the murder? You were right. We must have traced every breathing human being who was on the move in this area between nine and midnight. And all the time you were sitting upstairs, waiting patiently. We believe you finally slipped away when it was still dark, but not long before dawn. Perhaps a little after four, on a nice fresh summer morning. ... There's a quality people used to call arrogance of soul. It takes some people above themselves. It gives them the courage to die in torture. It takes other people below themselves. Then they can kill in torture. ... I think you're ready now to talk to me.

Dr Perryman (*after a pause*) Yes. I'm ready.

Briers presses the bell-push in the L wall and then goes and sits in the DL chair

Shingler and the Stenographer return, notebooks at the ready

Briers (*to Dr Perryman*) Take your time. (*He coughs*)

Dr Perryman (*gradually*) You don't have all that much, do you? I understand that you're retiring early. That cough? Naturally, before you break your staff, you want to end with a success. ... I've listened carefully, Chief Superintendent, to everything you've had to say. I've answered your questions to the best of my understanding. I've paid close attention to your various profiles of my character. Interesting, even flattering profiles. ... I have also followed your reconstruction of certain actions of mine. Now I am going to take a leaf out of your book and tell you that you are a most unusual man. We are, in fact, not unalike. ... In my profession I sometimes

tell an intelligent patient that I'll treat him like a specimen on the table
being examined by the two of us. Let's look at your case together like a
body on the table. Forget the psychological approach. Let's look at the
body of facts. What have we got? Yes, I was connected with Lady
Ashbrook. Yes, I did some business for her. Yes, some of the business
evaded some minor tax regulations. Yes, I was her executor after her death.
Yes, I was in a position to make a little money out of her. What else?
Nothing. That's it. The sum total. That's all we have in the way of fact. All
else is conjecture. No solid tissue. No concrete lesions. No *proof.* That's
what we need to complete a successful operation. Proof. *And that's what we
don't have. . . . (He gets up and crosses downstage)* And now if you'll forgive
me I really must get back to my patients. Oh, two minor matters. This
house. I consider that I've helped you as much as I reasonably can by
allowing you to use it as a base for your investigations, but as executor of
Lady Ashbrook's will I do have a certain responsibility to the beneficiaries.
If you have made no further progress in, say, a month from tonight, I shall
feel obliged to commence proceedings to obtain vacant possession.

Outside the windows it starts to rain

Briers And the other . . . minor matter?
Dr Perryman Occasionally I have a touch of sciatica in my right leg. Have
you ever had it? It makes walking rather painful, especially in the rain. I'd
be obliged if you could lay on transport. (*Hard, ruthless, totally dominant*)
Yes, I would like the police car that brought me here to take me home. *At
once, please!*

Briers glances at Shingler and gives an almost imperceptible nod

Shingler goes out with the Stenographer

Thank you.
Briers (*at length*) All papers relating to Lady Ashbrook's estate will be sent
to the Director of Public Prosecutions and the Inland Revenue.
Dr Perryman (*enjoying the mockery*) I admit I made . . . a modest killing. But
that kind of killing and the one you have in mind — that's another story,
isn't it? Good-night, Chief Superintendent. (*He starts out, limping slightly*)
Briers Doctor.

Dr Perryman stops

You did it. I know that you did it. What do you say, Doctor?
Dr Perryman (*at length, with utter confidence*) Prove it.

Dr Perryman exits

Black-out

EPILOGUE

The same. A cold winter's night

The drawing-room of the once again empty house is the same as it was in the Prologue with dust-sheets covering the furniture

The Lights come up on Briers, as before warmly wrapped up against the weather in his overcoat, sitting in the winged armchair. Humphrey, similarly attired, stands near the sofa

Humphrey You come here—how often?
Briers (*very still, immersed in his private thoughts*) Once, twice a week, perhaps.
Humphrey Illegally?
Briers Of course. The estate has had vacant possession since October.
Humphrey But still you come.
Briers The place haunts me. As I haunt it ... I know what happened here that night. Beyond all doubt. As though I'd been a fly upon the wall, I know it.

Pause

Humphrey (*watching him closely; with concern*) You said you expected a development. When you telephoned and asked me over. What development?
Briers (*rousing himself; with a certain excitement*) Bringing a murderer to justice is, to say the least, morally and socially desirable. You agree?
Humphrey Provided he's brought there by due process of law.
Briers The law and justice don't always ride tandem.
Humphrey Justice is mocked from time to time.
Briers By a too rigid adherence to the legal process, wouldn't you say?
Humphrey (*carefully*) By insuring that the benefit of the doubt goes to the accused.
Briers Suppose ... suppose a person were in a position to give justice a helping hand? Suppose, in a case where guilt was certain but proof lacking, it were possible to *provide* that proof? There could be a moral obligation, a duty, even—in certain exceptionally vicious circumstances, a clear and unavoidable duty—to do just that ... wouldn't you say?

Pause

Humphrey A clear and unavoidable duty to tamper with the course of justice?
Briers (*fast, eager*) In the name of justice.

Humphrey To undermine the law——

Briers The letter, not the spirit. To distort the truth in order to reveal it. To convict a murderer — as cold-hearted a killer as it's given to a man to be. What do you say?

Humphrey (*carefully*) I would say that to do that would be to commit a sort of murder oneself.

Briers (*gradually*) A sort of murder . . . all right. . . . Yes, all right . . . a sort of murder. . . . But a murder with an unspoken mandate from society. A murder in the name of a higher good. . . . Wouldn't you say?

Humphrey Whoever managed to persuade himself out of that would have to be a sick man.

Briers (*sharply*) Sick?

Humphrey Obsessed. Obsession is a sickness. Playing God is a sickness. Such a person would be playing God. Wouldn't *you* say?

Briers And what — do tell me — what were you playing on the island, when you pulled every dirty trick in the book?

Humphrey (*mercilessly*) I was a soldier fighting a war. You don't fight wars with a rulebook. You're a policeman keeping the peace. You can't do that without one.

Pause

Briers (*with a sudden smile, relaxing*) We all have our fantasies. I was just . . . flying an imaginary kite . . .

The telephone rings

(*Answering the telephone*) Briers. . . . (*He listens carefully. Then calmly*) Right. Get a warrant. Bring him in. No, on second thoughts, I'll bring him in myself. . . . Yes, I'm sure. I'll do it. Not without a certain relish. Oh — and, Norman — thanks. (*He hangs up. After a pause*) You never know your luck, do you?

Humphrey Luck?

Briers I don't have to tell you that police work is nine-tenths patience, one-tenth luck. . . . (*Gradually*) It seems they've found a suit . . . a man's grey worsted . . . buried in the garden of an empty house not half a mile from here. . . . Sewn into the lining are the doctor's initials. . . . By the way, it's stained with blood . . .

Pause

Humphrey (*quietly*) How did you know where to look?

Briers We had a tip-off.

Humphrey From whom?

Briers It was anonymous. We get them all the time.

Pause

Humphrey Why didn't he destroy it? I mean, if that was the suit he was wearing when he killed her——

Briers Oh, you don't doubt he killed her?

Humphrey Of course he killed her. But a blood-stained suit complete with initials, why bury it? Why not destroy it?

Pause

Briers You believe someone nicked that suit from the doctor's wardrobe one day when he was out attending to some bed of pain . . . smeared it with the appropriate blood group and planted it, in more senses than one, in that garden half a mile away. . . . That *is* what you're thinking, isn't it?

Pause

Humphrey (*at length*) What I'm thinking is not the question. The question is what he will say? And what he almost certainly will say is that this is your last case. That you desperately want to win it. That to make assurance double sure you've had him framed. That *you* planted a suit of his in that garden, appropriately doctored. . . . If — *when* that is put to you — what will be *your* answer? Frank?

Briers (*simply*) The same as his when I told him I knew he was a murderer. I'll say "*Prove it*". . . . And now, let's get out of here, shall we, before we freeze to death? (*He starts out, stops and turns suddenly on Humphrey*) You want to know the *real* question? The sixty-four thousand dollar conundrum of our life and times? (*Deliberately, but with great force and feeling*) How long can a society survive that still believes life is a cricket match, to be played in strict accordance with the rules? While those who would destroy that society believe there *are* no rules; that in a world where violence, kidnap, hijack, random terror in the streets and skies, assassination are a daily diet, nothing's sacred, nothing's barred; that the end justifies the means — the most brutal, pitiless, murdering means on earth? How long . . .? I'll tell you how long. *Not very* . . . Unless, at the eleventh hour, this country gets it through its skull that the game its enemies are playing, it, too, can play — and, if driven to it, with an even baser and more ruthless dedication . . .

Pause. Humphrey goes to the door to exit

Humphrey (*turning*) You throw away the rule-book — albeit in a just cause — you add one more brick to the building of the ultimate degenerate and corrupt society. Is such a society worthy of survival?

Pause

Briers (*finally*) I don't know . . . I don't know. . . . I only know it's a profound need of society to take its revenge on those who offend its deepest instincts. You know who said that? Ralph Perryman, MD, FRCS (*He looks up at the wall, at the portrait; softly*) Rest in peace . . .
Humphrey Will *you* . . .?

Short pause

Humphrey exits

Briers turns to the door but Humphrey has gone. The detective turns to face the audience and stands, his face a blank, without expression

Black-out

CURTAIN

FURNITURE AND PROPERTY LIST

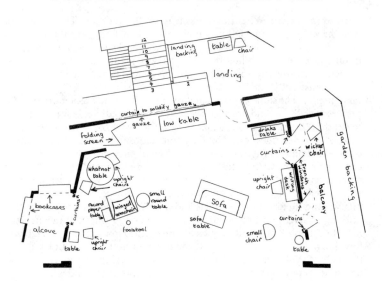

PROLOGUE

On stage: NB. All items of furniture are covered by dust-sheets

Landing table. *On it:* telephone, ornaments

Landing chair

Drinks table. *On it:* ice-bowl containing ice, soda siphon, bottles of soft
   drinks (including bitter lemon and Coca-cola), decanter of brandy,
   bottle of whisky, various glasses

Low table. *On it:* ornaments

Folding screen

Whatnot table. *On it:* table lamp (practical), ornaments, vase of flowers,
   clock

4 upright chairs

Winged armchair

Small round table. *On it:* books, magazines etc.

Small table. *On it:* record player

Small round footstool

Occasional table. *On it:* ornaments

Books on alcove shelves

Alcove curtains open

Sofa. *On it:* cushions

Low sofa table
Bell push in L wall
Round occasional table. *On it:* ornaments
Small chair. *On it:* bouquet of lilies, cushion
Writing-desk. *On it:* telephone, table lamp, framed photograph of Loseby
    in uniform. *In pigeon-hole section:* wad of currency. *Under desk:* toolbox
    containing screwdrivers etc. *Above desk:* large twenties portrait of Lady
    Ashbrook with attached portrait light (practical)
Wicker chair on balcony
French windows closed
Window curtains open

Personal: **Briers:** watch, reading glasses (used throughout the play), address book

ACT I

Scene 1

Strike: All dust sheets

Set: French windows open

Off stage: Vase for lilies (**Susan**)

Personal: **Dr Perryman:** watch, pocket diary, wallet
           Lady Ashbrook: handbag
           Humphrey: wallet

ACT I

Scene 2

Strike: **Lady Ashbrook**'s handbag and 2 glasses
           Vase of lilies from US table
           Flowers from vase on whatnot table

Set: Substitute flowers in vase on whatnot table

Re-set: Upright chairs overturned
           Sofa moved
           Tables overturned, moved out of position etc.
           Alcove curtains pulled down

Check: French windows open
           Window curtains open

Off stage: Briefcase (**Briers**)
           Black case. *In it:* pair of surgical gloves, anal thermometer, polythene bag,
           cassette recorder, notebook, pen (**Professor Morgan**)

Cup of coffee on silver salver **(Maria)**
Plastic sheet **(Tanner)**
Folded copy of *The Times* **(Humphrey)**
Camera, flash unit, etc. **(Photographer)**

Personal: **Tanner:** walkie-talkie radio, notebook
              Shingler: notebook, pen

ACT I

Scene 3

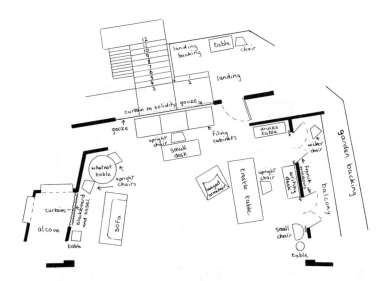

Strike: Folding screen
              Low table US
              Sofa table
              Small round footstool
              Small table with record-player
              Small round table

Set: 3 filing cabinets. *On them:* box files, papers, index files etc.
              Large noticeboard. *On it:* large map of London with various coloured
                  areas, other papers
              Small desk. *On it:* 3 telephones, typewriter, paper, **Dr Perryman**'s statement
                  (for **Shingler**)
              Trestle table. *On it:* intercom telephone, writing pads, pens, pencils, bottle
                  of cough mixture and glass. *Beside it:* wastepaper bin
              Files, papers and extra telephone on writing-desk

Notes in writing-desk drawer
Large blackboard and easel. *On blackboard:* detailed map of SW London
  with house ringed in red, chalked words "Belgravia", "Chelsea",
  "Pimlico", "Victoria", "Lambeth", etc. with number of houses visited
  by each. *On easel:* cloth, chalk
Dr Perryman's bag on sofa

Re-set: Sofa R
Winged armchair C
Small chair against DL wall
Alcove curtains closed
Upright chair from DR to UC behind small desk
Upright chair at writing-desk behind trestle table
Briers's briefcase under black-board

Check: French windows open
Window curtains open

Off stage: Tray of food **(Policewoman)**
Piece of paper **(Shingler)**
Folded newspaper **(Humphrey)**

Personal: **Dr Perryman:** pocket diary
Humphrey: pen
Briers: handkerchief

ACT II

Scene 1

Strike: Tray of food from trestle table

Set: Hammer in toolbox for Scene 2

Personal: **Shingler:** notebook, pen
Susan: multi-coloured shoulder bag containing lipstick and mirror,
  diamond engagement ring

ACT II

Scene 2

Strike: 3 filing-cabinets
Large noticeboard
Small desk
Trestle table and wastepaper bin
Large blackboard and easel
Files, 2nd telephone from writing-desk (leaving papers)
Vase of flowers from whatnot table

Re-set:	Sofa C
	Winged armchair DR
	Upright chair from UC to DR
	Upright table from trestle table to writing-desk
	Small armchair DL as before
	Bottle of cough mixture and glass on writing-desk
	Alcove curtains open
	French windows closed

Set: Folding screen
Low table US
Sofa table
Small round footstool for winged armchair
Small round table L of winged armchair
Small table R of winged armchair. *On it:* record player

Check: Window curtains open

Off stage: Notebook, pencil **(Stenographer)**
Tray. *On it:* 2 mugs of tea, sugar bowl and spoons **(Policewoman)**

Personal: **Dr Perryman:** watch, small bottle of pills in pocket

DURING 1st BLACK-OUT

Set: Tray on small round table L of winged armchair. *On it:* remains of light meal
Vase of flowers on whatnot table

Re-set: French windows closed
US curtain backing gauze open

Off stage: Medical bag **(Dr Perryman)**

DURING 2nd BLACK-OUT

Strike: Tray on small round table
Vase of flowers from whatnot table
Medical bag

Re-set: French windows closed
Window curtains open
US curtain backing gauze closed

Off stage: Notebook, pencil **(Stenographer)**
Notebook, pen **(Shingler)**

EPILOGUE

On stage: Dust-sheets covering all items of furniture

LIGHTING PLOT

Practical fittings required: wall-brackets, portrait light, table lamp UR
Interior. The same scene throughout

PROLOGUE. Winter's night

To open: Moonlight effect from windows with landing area lit

Cue 1   **Briers** turns on portrait light   (Page 1)
              Snap on portrait light and covering spot

Cue 2   **Briers** turns on other lights   (Page 1)
              Snap on wall-brackets and bring up general interior lighting

Cue 3   **Briers:** "... during a heatwave ..."   (Page 2)
              Fade to Black-out. Quickly bring up opening effect for Scene 1

ACT I, Scene 1. Summer evening 6.30 p.m.

To open: Early evening sunshine effect through french windows

Cue 4   **Lady Ashbrook** downs her brandy at a gulp   (Page 13)
              Black-out

ACT I, Scene 2. Summer, early morning

To open: Bright early morning sunshine effect through french windows

Cue 5   **Briers:** "It hadn't occurred to me."   (Page 25)
              Black-out

ACT I, Scene 3. Summer's day

To open: Bright sunshine effect through french windows

No cues

ACT II, Scene 1. Summer's day

To open: Bright sunshine effect through french windows

Cue 6   **Briers** and **Humphrey** face each other   (Page 42)
              Fade to Black-out

ACT II, Scene 2. Autumn, early evening

To open: Dusk effect through french windows increasing gradually

Cue 7   As **Briers** begins speech: "You didn't call here ..."   (Page 48)
              Fade to spot on **Briers**

Cue 8   **Briers:** "... for what you had to do ..."   (Page 49)
              Start fade to Black-out

| *Cue* 9 | When ready | (Page 49) |

Bring up lighting to give heavy shadow effect with UR *table lamp and covering spot on and dim lighting on landing section and stairs to upper floor*

| *Cue* 10 | **Dr Perryman** enters the drawing-room | (Page 49) |

Fade lighting on landing section and stairs

| *Cue* 11 | The "Emperor Waltz" plays fortissimo | (Page 52) |

Black-out

| *Cue* 12 | As music fades | (Page 53) |

Bring up spot on **Briers**

| *Cue* 13 | **Briers:** "... the impression of an intruder ..." | (Page 53) |

Gradually bring up autumn dusk lighting as before

| *Cue* 14 | **Dr Perryman** exits | (Page 54) |

Black-out

EPILOGUE. Winter's night

To open: Wall-brackets, portrait light, landing area lit with moonlight effect through french windows

| *Cue* 15 | **Briers** stands, facing front | (Page 57) |

Black-out

EFFECTS PLOT

Please read the notice on page iv concerning the use of copyright material. Strauss's *Emperor Waltz* plays at the end of every scene

NB. During the scenes which take place in summer, from time to time, in counterpoint to the action, bird-song, the hum of distant traffic and the gentle relaxing sounds of summer in London are heard

PROLOGUE

No cues

ACT I

Cue 1	**Lady Ashbrook:** "You see, you dissemble already." *Clock strikes the three-quarter*	(Page 5)
Cue 2	**Susan:** "Thanks." (*She starts out*) *Distant bell rings*	(Page 9)
Cue 3	**Loseby:** "It couldn't matter bloody less!" *Telephone rings*	(Page 11)
Cue 4	**Lady Ashbrook:** "Or has it stopped now?" *Ping of telephone receiver being replaced*	(Page 11)
Cue 5	Black-out to end SCENE 2 *Strauss's "Emperor Waltz" plays. Eventually drowned by police-car siren building to a climax. When ready, cut suddenly*	(Page 13)
Cue 6	**Photographer** exits through the alcove *Camera click and flash. Continuing intermittently until* **Photographer** *enters the drawing-room*	(Page 20)
Cue 7	**Shingler** goes out *Telephone rings*	(Page 22)
Cue 8	**Dr Perryman:** "... I must go." *Intercom buzz*	(Page 28)

ACT II

Cue 9	**Shingler:** "Who *were* you waiting for?" *Intercom buzz*	(Page 38)
Cue 10	The Lights come up on **Lady Ashbrook** in her chair *Record of Strauss's "Emperor Waltz"*	(Page 49)

EPILOGUE

MADE AND PRINTED IN GREAT BRITAIN BY
LATIMER TREND & COMPANY LTD PLYMOUTH
MADE IN ENGLAND